PUFFIN BOOKS

The
Promise

The True Story of a Family in the Holocaust

Eva Schloss lives in north London and has been married
to Zvi for over fifty years. They have three grown-up
daughters and five grandchildren. Eva regularly visits
schools, universities and other institutions to talk about
her experiences during the Holocaust. A play, *And Then
They Came for Me: Remembering the World of Anne Frank*
by James Still, deals with the lives of Eva and her
posthumous stepsister, Anne Frank, and other teenagers
in the Holocaust. It has been performed all over the USA
and in many other countries, including a performance by
children and young people in London in 2005 to mark
the liberation of Auschwitz.

Eva is a trustee of the Anne Frank Trust in London.

The True Story of a Family
in the Holocaust

The Promise

Eva Schloss
and Barbara Powers

Illustrated by Sophie Yaron
(aged ten)

PUFFIN

PUFFIN BOOKS

Published by the Penguin Group
Penguin Books Ltd, 80 Strand, London WC2R ORL, England
Penguin Group (USA) Inc., 375 Hudson Street, New York, New York 10014, USA
Penguin Group (Canada), 90 Eglinton Avenue East, Suite 700, Toronto, Ontario, Canada M4P 2Y3
(a division of Pearson Penguin Canada Inc.)
Penguin Ireland, 25 St Stephen's Green, Dublin 2, Ireland (a division of Penguin Books Ltd)
Penguin Group (Australia), 250 Camberwell Road, Camberwell, Victoria 3124, Australia
(a division of Pearson Australia Group Pty Ltd)
Penguin Books India Pvt Ltd, 11 Community Centre, Panchsheel Park, New Delhi – 110 017, India
Penguin Group (NZ), cnr Airborne and Rosedale Roads, Albany, Auckland 1310, New Zealand
(a division of Pearson New Zealand Ltd)
Penguin Books (South Africa) (Pty) Ltd, 24 Sturdee Avenue, Rosebank, Johannesburg 2196, South Africa

Penguin Books Ltd, Registered Offices: 80 Strand, London WC2R ORL, England

www.penguin.com

First published 2006

6

Text copyright © Eva Schloss and Barbara Powers, 2006
Illustrations copyright © Sophie Yaron (granddaughter of Eva Schloss), 2006
All rights reserved

The moral right of the author and illustrator has been asserted

Set in Bembo 11.5/15pt
Typeset by Palimpsest Book Production Limited, Polmont, Stirlingshire
Made and printed in England by Clays Ltd, St Ives plc

British Library Cataloguing in Publication Data
A CIP catalogue record for this book is available from the British Library

ISBN-13: 978-0-141-32081-6
ISBN-10: 0-141-32081-8

www.greenpenguin.co.uk

Mixed Sources
Product group from well-managed
forests and other controlled sources
www.fsc.org Cert no. SA-COC-1592
© 1996 Forest Stewardship Council

Penguin Books is committed to a sustainable future
for our business, our readers and our planet.
The book in your hands is made from paper
certified by the Forest Stewardship Council.

*To my brother, Heinz, who died so young. He showed
me how dear and how close a sibling can be. I have
never ceased missing him.*
Eva Schloss

*In celebration of my son, Bobby Powers, and father, Raymond
Krahe. Although they died in 1986, we remain connected
in infinite ways . . . ways as brilliant as the colours of
autumn, ways that inspire my storytelling.*
Barbara Powers

Acknowledgements

We gratefully recognize the love and encouragement of our families, which continues to sustain us. We wish to acknowledge and thank Helen Levene, our editor, for her genuine caring throughout this project. Her advice and personal consideration during each stage of the writing process served as an inspiration. Most importantly, she helped us in getting to the heart of the story.

Also our deepest thanks to Helen's colleagues at Puffin Books for their support and publication of *The Promise*.

A long-held dream has now come true.

Eva and Barbara

Contents

Introduction

As I look back more than sixty years to the early part of my life, the pictures in my memory are crystal clear. Many reveal happy faces: my family gathered around the supper table; my friends in a game of rounders on a summer's afternoon; my father in the mountains; my brother, Heinz, with a paintbrush in his hands; and grandfather at the piano with me on his lap. I can see flowers in our garden, presents on my birthday and new shoes for my growing feet. I hear laughter, wonderful music and my mother's comforting words.

The past also reveals events that are hard to believe, yet all are true. My family lived during the Second World War, caught in the Nazi march across Europe. While I was a young child, I witnessed terrible destruction and cruelty. Unfortunately, millions of other children and families suffered as well. My mother and I were among the few who survived. My father and only brother were not.

This is the story of my family, an account of the events that tore us from our home in Austria and filled the world with terror and suffering. It is also a remembrance of my father's wisdom and zest for life, my mother's positive outlook in every circumstance and my brother's artistic gifts, evidenced in the paintings and poetry he left behind. They have sustained me through the worst of times, even when we were separated.

I hope through this book you will be moved to share kindness and tolerance with others; appreciate your parents, brothers, sisters and extended family, realizing that your time together is precious; develop your talents to make the world a better place; appreciate the freedom that was won for you through great sacrifice; and value each day.

1.

Born into a Loving Family

Our parents always told us that their marriage was made in heaven. Elfriede Markovits, our cheerful and beautiful mother, whom we called Mutti, made a lovely bride in her long, flowing, white gown, her soft, gentle face glowing with happiness. Her groom was Erich Geiringer, a handsome young businessman with deep blue eyes and an inviting smile. He looked quite polished in his smart wedding suit, but everyone easily sensed his warmth and charm.

During their first years together they didn't have a care in the world. Life was exciting and free from worry. They lived in Vienna, Austria, an important and beautiful city on the majestic Danube River, at the foot of the Wiener Wald (the Vienna Woods). Adorned with Renaissance and baroque architecture, imperial palaces with formal gardens, famous art museums, exquisite theatres and opera houses, Vienna provided endless cultural and social events.

Erich and Elfriede, Fritzi for short, and their many friends planned fun outings to the mountains, lakes and the heart of the city. They enjoyed working hard at making a home and building a future. And they dreamed of having children who could share in their happiness.

In 1926 the Geiringers welcomed their first child, Heinz Felix. Mutti and Pappy described him as a sweet and easy-going baby, yet Heinz wore a studious look even at a young age. Pappy said that his piercing eyes often caused them to wonder what he was thinking.

Heinz didn't get upset easily, but at age three he had an experience which clearly had a lasting effect on him. Mutti and Pappy had sent him to stay with our grandparents without any explanation. Although he loved to stay with Grandfather Rudolf and Grandmother Helen, he must have wondered where his Mutti and Pappy had gone. In his absence, on 11 May 1929, I was born. Of course, I had no awareness of Heinz's trauma, but I was told later that it caused him to stutter. This frustrated him greatly, but for me it was a reminder that we were meant to be together.

On my first birthday Pappy gathered us for a photograph. I cuddled in Mutti's arms, looking directly at the camera with wide and curious eyes. Heinz stood close by Mutti's side with his little hands crossed on her lap, while Mutti radiated a look of contentment and joy. Pappy adjusted Heinz's collar and tie, then stepped back, paused to gaze at his beautiful family with pride and exhilaration and snapped the shutter. A precious moment was captured for posterity.

Like Mutti and Pappy, Heinz and I adored each other. We made a unique pair: Heinz, clever and sensitive, and me, practical and daring. Our interests and ambitions were poles apart, but we had a similar thirst for adventure and found ways to make learning fun. Heinz found excitement in books, while I craved the thrill of new experiences.

We challenged our parents in different ways but admired and appreciated them just the same.

Unlike Heinz, I didn't grow at a normal pace and Mutti and Pappy always worried about my weight.

'You are far too skinny,' Mutti said, placing an extra helping of potatoes and vegetables on my plate. She insisted that I eat red cabbage, spinach and a varied diet that didn't include any of the foods I liked. I ate my meals very slowly and had to sit at the table until every last morsel was gone. As a result, I sat for what seemed like hours, convinced that these demands were completely unreasonable for a perfectly healthy and energetic girl like me.

Heinz rescued me from boredom by whispering promises in my ear. 'I'll tell you some good stories tonight,' he said, going on about the book he had been reading. 'Remember how Winnetou is going to talk to the Indian chief about going on a hunt with Old Shatterhand? Well, wait until you hear what happens.'

The time passed quickly as pictures of the story played in my mind's eye. Then, later that night, I listened happily as Heinz retold all of my favourite stories.

Despite the special meals, I didn't grow any faster. Mutti took me to a doctor twice a week for treatments to improve my appetite. The nurse gave me a pair of dark glasses to wear which I thought were stupid, but Heinz said I looked like a glamorous film star in them. Then I had to sit under a special ultraviolet lamp that shone on my face and had a very strong smell of disinfectant that I detested.

When this didn't help, Pappy took me to a mountain resort called Semmering, about an hour's train ride from our home. He chattered non-stop the entire trip in his nervousness about leaving me in a strange place. I stayed in a children's home with other children needing treatment, and the nurses and doctors who were taking care of us. Every evening a nurse came in with a bottle of cod liver oil. When I saw her approaching my stomach immediately tightened. She poured out a full tablespoon. 'Now, Evi, it's not that bad,' she said.

I pressed my lips closed while she tried to cajole me, ultimately warning me of the consequences for my lack of cooperation. Finally I swallowed the cod liver oil and got sick. The nurse became very cross.

After this ordeal all the children had to have a cup of cocoa that was very hot and had a skin on top. This made me sick as well, so the nurse called my parents and said the children's home didn't think that I would benefit from this treatment. Pappy came to fetch me back, and in due time I grew.

Pappy had boundless energy like me, which resulted in high expectations of his children.

'You must never be afraid,' he said to us at a very young age.

Once he placed me up high on a wardrobe, stood back, held out his arms and invited me to jump. My brow tightened and the tears started to pool in my eyes. Pappy looked back at me with a knowing smile. In that instant his strength seemed to wash over me and my fears disappeared. I leaped into his arms with all the trust in the world, and when he caught me we laughed with joy.

Pappy didn't hesitate to give Heinz and me new challenges, assuming that we would learn to rely on our own instincts and strengths to pull through. Mutti was mortified the day he tossed me into a large swimming pool eight feet deep. She flapped her hands anxiously, calling out a string of warnings while I moved with ease, like a giant sea turtle. When Pappy retrieved me I asked for more.

Heinz sat off to the side and shook his head, saying repeatedly, 'No thank you, Pappy,' every time Pappy glanced his way.

I worshipped Pappy and tried to be just like him. He often took us all hiking on day trips in the foothills of the Alps. Pappy gave Heinz and me our own backpacks to carry, filled with snacks for energy and extra clothes for protection. We played 'follow the leader' through the rough mountain terrain, usually with Pappy or me at the helm. I didn't complain when my feet got tired, but instead asked Pappy if I could go barefoot. He readily approved with a few words of caution. Surprisingly, the sharp rocks didn't hurt my tender soles. Instead, I rather enjoyed feeling the texture of the earth.

Pappy found pockets of white edelweiss tucked in the high rocks. 'Look, a precious treasure,' he called out. 'We must have a closer look.'

He anchored a rope, then demonstrated how we could climb up by pulling ourselves up the cliffs. It looked easy as he lifted his own weight with strong hands and arms and a wide smile on his face. Then Pappy challenged us to give it a try.

Before Mutti and Heinz even had a chance to decline I jumped up shouting, 'Can I go first?' Pappy agreed since no one else showed an interest in participating.

'Be careful,' Mutti called out a thousand times. Then she waited anxiously for us to climb back down, while Heinz read a few more pages in his latest favourite book. Pappy and I returned victorious, having also discovered patches of the red and pink Alpine rose. I chattered on and on about it the entire trip home.

On longer holidays we travelled further and stayed overnight at country inns filled with quaint, wooden handmade furniture. I thought that the stuffed heads of wild boars mounted on the walls looked fascinating and I gave each one a name. Heinz laughed when he found out. In the evenings the local farmers gathered to play their accordions and dance. We wore the Tyrolean costumes Mutti had bought for each of us. I felt as if we belonged, especially when we joined in the clapping. My heart beat fast when I heard the first notes of my favourite dance. The men kicked up their legs, clapping over and under and around each other, even pretending to smack one another. Heinz and I laughed until we cried.

'I love Austria,' I said to Mutti and Pappy later that night before drifting off to sleep. 'Me too,' Heinz said.

In 1933 Heinz contracted a terrible illness. No one knew what caused his sudden fever, and no matter what Mutti did it wouldn't subside. Heinz lay in his bed for hours, sleeping or staring into space. I tried making up stories like he did for me, but he seemed lost in another world, not caring about anything, not even his books.

At long last Mutti and Pappy found a specialist who explained that Heinz's tonsils had been very infected and poison had entered his bloodstream. They arranged to have his tonsils removed, and finally he began to recover. However, the sickness affected his eyesight, and although he visited many specialists and hospitals, he eventually became blind in one eye.

The whole shocking ordeal concerned all of us. Mutti and Pappy felt helpless watching Heinz suffer and worried frantically that an accident would cause him to lose the sight in his other eye. Heinz also constantly feared becoming totally blind, which would leave him unable to read.

All the while I missed my brother. I just wanted him to act like himself. When at last he felt like talking and doing ordinary things again, I could hardly leave his side.

While I continued to love challenges, Heinz remained cautious and timid.

'Heinz must learn to face his fears,' Pappy insisted.

This statement resulted in arguments with Mutti. She glanced at Heinz with a mother's heart and found it hard to agree that he should be expected to act contrary to his gentle nature. At the same time, she understood Pappy's concerns. He wanted his son to toughen up so that he would be able to endure life's difficulties.

Ultimately, Mutti supported Pappy and encouraged Heinz to become more active and try out new things. She also looked out for my best interests. I was expected to spend time reading each day, look presentable with my hair brushed and my clothes neat, act politely and be well-mannered, especially at the supper table. Heinz and I listened to constant reminders about how to hold our cutlery properly. This often led to pouting and complaints, but years later I appreciated the high standards that our parents set.

Heinz read voraciously. He travelled everywhere in the stories of Jules Verne: under the sea, to the centre of the earth, to the moon and around the world. He encountered cannibals and sea monsters, sunless seas and regions of eternal snows. I often tried to get his attention when he was reading, but his face was buried in his book. His hands gripped the pages, his body folded up in the chair as if he were tucked in another place, and I suspected that he didn't hear a single word I said. Eventually he would look up and explain to me how the crashing waves of the sea resounded in his head as the ship was going down. Then I would get so engrossed in the tale that I'd forget all about what I wanted to tell him.

Heinz also loved music, a gift inherited from Mutti's father. Whenever we visited Grandfather Rudolph he invited Heinz to sit beside him on the piano stool while he played magnificent virtuoso music. Heinz studied him closely, following Grandfather's hands as they flew over the keyboard in complicated patterns. I became dizzy trying to watch them.

Grandfather played by ear, without any score, sometimes with his eyes closed.

'How do you do that?' Heinz asked.

'I find the music in my head, my hands, my ears and my heart,' Grandfather explained. 'When I was a young student I refused to play with sheet music, and so the piano teacher was no longer willing to give me lessons. I may have been a bit too stubborn for my own good, but I was no less determined to learn.'

I was stubborn and determined too, but I had no musical talent. Still, Grandfather shared with me just the same. He lifted me up on to his lap and played games that went right along with the melodies. The sounds came to life like characters in a story. I laughed and asked for more, and grew to love many styles of music.

Heinz wanted desperately to learn. He began piano lessons that continued for many years. His obedience and diligence served him well, and he became accomplished like Grandfather and Mutti. Only Mutti always made sure her music books were open.

Heinz also played guitar and accordion, which made him very popular among our friends. Many people said he was 'a natural'. The notes seemed to come without any effort, but I saw the hours and hours he sat practising different strums and patterns.

'It is a labour of love,' Mutti said with a smile.

Pappy loved music too, and often called us together for a special concert of 'sleeping' music. He placed the gramophone right in the middle of the living-room floor and put on a recording called the 'Trout Quintet' by the Austrian composer, Franz Schubert. We gathered round, stretched out on the carpet, our heads in the middle near the speaker. The gentle lull of the melody felt like a rocking cradle.

'I'm floating off on a dream,' I announced.

'Shh,' Heinz responded.

The beautiful music and nearness of my family gave me a sense of perfect contentment.

Grandmother Helen and Grandfather Rudolph lived nearby. Every Sunday morning Grandfather came to fetch me for an outing to the local inn. We walked hand in hand while I listened to him tell stories of his early days. His friends waited for us at tables reserved just for the grandfathers and me. The waitress brought us a typical Austrian breakfast with steaming goulash soup. As she poured it carefully in our bowls from a big, shiny silver-plated pot I laughed at the reflection of our happy faces. The grandfathers invited me to talk about what I had been learning and the fun things I had been doing. They seemed very interested in everything I had to say. I always looked forward to these special times.

Aunt Sylvi, Mutti's only sister, and Aunt Blanca, Pappy's only sister, also lived just a short distance away with their families. They were our favourite playmates, along with the grandchildren of Grandmother's three siblings, and Pappy's numerous cousins. Unfortunately, Pappy's parents, Grandfather David and Grandmother Hermine, had died before we were born. He missed them terribly, and often mentioned Grandmother's cooking and Grandfather's laugh. He told us many stories about them and we felt a close kinship even though we had never met.

My closest cousin, Gaby, the same age as me, became my very best friend. Unlike my fair colouring, Gaby had dark hair and dark brown eyes. Her mother, Aunt Blanca, decided that she couldn't possibly go through childbirth more than once, so Gaby remained an only child, and often felt very lonely. Consequently, she ended up spending many afternoons at our home where there was always something going on. We made her feel like a sister, including her in our plans and schemes, and even in our bickering.

Sometimes we visited Gaby's home in a new neighbourhood on the outskirts of the city. Beyond her back garden the open country stretched until it met the sky. We often climbed over the gate to explore the wild areas. Once I convinced the neighbourhood children to meet Gaby and me at a big pile of stones and rubble, the ruins of a castle. We were having great fun, making up stories of kings and queens, when I heard Pappy's voice.

'Evi, Gaby, children, this place is dangerous. You could get hurt.'

Pappy talked to me about setting a good example, suspecting that I was the ringleader of the escapade. Heinz put his arm around Gaby and shared a bit of big brotherly advice about safety and caution.

I wasn't in trouble for long and we returned to the house to play one of my favourite games called 'Quartet'. We passed cards around the table to make sets of four, each set a family of a different nationality with a father, mother, girl and boy. We liked trying to pronounce the names.

'I have completed the French family: Daniel, Madeleine, Pierre and Nicole,' I announced. 'Oh, I wish I had been named Nicole. It sounds so lovely and stylish.'

Heinz told us about the customs of each nation, which gave me a good feeling about people all over the world.

Some of the distant relatives owned a health spa near Vienna called Baden bei Wien. Often they invited us to visit. Pappy enjoyed strolling through the beautiful park inside the compound and being spoiled with the delicious, exotic meals that were served. Mutti especially liked soaking in the large pool of warm water that bubbled up from the natural spring because it helped her rheumatism. I agreed that it felt wonderful, but the sulphur in the water smelled like rotten eggs and nearly made me sick. It was so strong that Heinz and I could detect it in the air before we arrived at the resort.

When I began to make a fuss about the awful odour, Heinz teased me. 'Look at Evi's face. It's beginning to turn green,' he said, laughing. 'Just pretend it's something else, like exotic spices, then it won't be so bad.'

We appreciated the fact that our relatives lived near, and became accustomed to seeing one or more of them almost daily. Mutti consulted with her mother and sister on every topic, and together they planned family gatherings with great detail and thoughtfulness. Pappy engaged in fun activities with the children. Heinz spent hours making music with Grandfather Rudolph. I took gymnastic lessons from Mutti's cousin Litty, who helped me recognize my positive traits and referred to me as one of her favourite pupils. She called me a '*Schlangen-mensch*' (snake-person) because of my suppleness and flexibility, and often asked me to demonstrate my acrobatics to others. Pappy was particularly proud of this accomplishment and so was I. Though Heinz and I only had each other as siblings, we felt very fortunate to belong to such a large family.

Sophie Aaron

2.

Surprised by the Joys of Life

Pappy often surprised us with new ideas for his job, our home, holiday plans, ways to make life easier and more fun. He talked about the modern machinery being invented by people in England and America, and how Europe was much slower to make changes. In 1935, to our great amazement, he came home with a brand-new car. Heinz was the first to notice.

'Mutti, there's a car outside our house. Who could it be? Is anyone coming to visit? Oh, look, Mutti, Evi, it's Pappy!' he said, and then he grabbed my hand and together we ran outside.

At first Mutti was incredulous. 'Erich, what have you gone and done?' she said, somewhat sternly, and yet with a gleeful look on her face.

It was the first car anyone in the family had owned, and we were overjoyed. On weekends Pappy drove us into the mountains on winding roads, calling out commands that we look this way and that at the spectacular views. Mutti screamed at each sharp bend and hairpin turn, while Heinz and I sat in the back seat, clutching each other with fear and excitement.

'Can you see that, Evi? Can you see all the way down to the bottom of the cliff? The barns and houses look like toy blocks,' Heinz said, his eyes wide and his fingers squeezing my arm so tightly I feared my bones would break. All the while we giggled with delight, and Pappy's smile reached from ear to ear.

Mutti preferred family gatherings at home to Pappy's adventurous outings. On Friday nights, when the sun set low in the sky and Pappy was about to arrive home for supper, Mutti called out for Heinz and me to come and help her prepare the table for the Sabbath. I skipped down the long hallway and around the corner into the dining room with Heinz following behind me, a book still open in his hands. We helped lay the table with our best silver cutlery, pretty china plates and carefully starched and pressed linen napkins. I set the tall candles in the candlesticks.

'There! Doesn't everything look lovely,' I said, wrapping my arms around Mutti's waist.

We celebrated the Sabbath in this way every single week, and it never lost its brilliance. Our appreciation for our Jewish way of life began at home as well as in school with our enthusiastic religious studies teacher. Religious education was compulsory in every school. Since Austria was mainly a Catholic country, the Jewish children had to leave the classroom for separate lessons with a Jewish teacher. We learned about all the Jewish festivals, and Mutti and Pappy were thrilled when Heinz and I practised them at home. We studied the Jewish alphabet, and while I could recite the letters, I never really learned to read Hebrew. Heinz, on the other hand, became quite good at it. When he recited prayers in Hebrew I thought his voice sounded distinguished and wise.

Our large extended family gathered every year to celebrate the festival of Passover, when the Jews were freed from slavery in Egypt. As children we enjoyed the storytelling in the first part of the evening, especially Heinz, who was fascinated with Jewish history. We also looked forward to the special meal, including our favourite matzo ball soup. Pappy explained the symbolic meaning of all the foods passed around the table, and together we gave thanks and praise to God for liberating the Jewish people. After the meal the adults continued praying for what seemed like hours. The older children became rather restless while the younger ones dropped off to a peaceful sleep. But eventually everyone joined in singing the well-known Hebrew songs, and we ended the evening with great rejoicing.

During the festival of Hanukkah we remembered how the Jews made the Temple of Jerusalem fit again for holy service after it had been used to worship the Greek gods, and how the small amount of oil they found for the temple lamp miraculously lasted eight days. To symbolize this we lit a candle on the menorah for eight days in a row after sunset. We sang a special song, had special foods, like fried potato latkes and doughnuts, played games and received small gifts.

We liked to talk about our Jewish holidays and celebrations, bar mitzvahs and wedding rituals with many of our Christian friends. In turn, they talked about Christmas, Easter, baptisms and other religious celebrations. We never considered our differences a problem. We joined our fellow Austrians each year on 5 December to celebrate the feast of St Nicholas and Black Peter with parties, games and presents. We were proud of our countrymen and women, and happy with our homeland and traditions.

Our family was not rich, but we did have many comforts. Like most middle-class families, we had domestic help. Jobs were very hard to find, so people were willing to work in exchange for a room, board and a small wage. We had a maid who did all the shopping and cooking. She didn't use any recipes, but knew from memory how to prepare the complicated dishes, scrumptious dumplings and elaborate desserts. She lived in a small room behind out kitchen, and I often hid there when playing hide-and-seek with my friend Martin.

Every family sat down to their main meal at lunchtime between noon and two o'clock. Fathers came home from work and the students were sent home from school. In the evening we ate a small meal of sausage or semolina that was always lumpy. Sometimes I complained and Mutti sent me to stand in the corner next to a bentwood chair. I traced my finger around the circular pattern on the seat, chanting over and over, '. . . and I'm not going to apologize, and I'm not going to apologize'. Eventually I learned not to let such little things bother me.

We had other helpers: a lady who came in every week to do the washing and a seamstress who mended the bed linen and altered our clothes. Most of our garments were handed down from relatives and something often needed to be shortened or lengthened. I had great fun rummaging through a box of clothes, strolling back and forth from the living room to put on a fashion show for Pappy. At that point in our lives I believed with great certainty that any problem that came our way could be solved, and all our needs would be easily taken care of.

In the winter Heinz and I had to wear long woollen stockings with suspender belts, which we hated. We tried all kind of tricks to get out of it, hiding the stockings, claiming that they needed to be laundered, even pretending that we weren't allowed to wear them to school. One morning I rubbed the scratchy fabric across my skin until it became red and looked like I was developing a rash. How wonderful it would have been to have had an allergic reaction! But Mutti didn't believe it for a second.

One day Pappy surprised us with a carload of shoes from his factory. They were not in pairs and Pappy instructed Heinz and me to sort them out. We covered the floor of our large entrance from corner to corner and turned our task into a game. Heinz became a salesman and I pretended to shop for shoes.

Mutti and Pappy smiled at our play-acting, and then turned their attention towards more serious concerns. Pappy's shoe factory began to fail. Despite Pappy's efficiency and hard work and the dedication of his employees, sales continued to drop off. This didn't come as too great a surprise since Austria and all of Europe had fallen into an economic depression, and we knew many families with fathers out of work.

Heinz and I also noticed that our parents listened more closely to the radio news broadcasts and talked with a different sound in their voices about other problems. We didn't understand what was happening; we just knew that our parents seemed greatly distressed.

We learned eventually that Germany, the neighbouring country, had appointed a new government leader named Adolf Hitler, head of the National Socialist German Workers' Party, known as the Nazi party. He spoke to the German people with powerful assurances, promising jobs, a new order and a bright future. At the time, one out of three workers was unemployed. Political unrest in villages and towns brought constant fighting and frequent killings. People were hungry, afraid and discouraged. Hitler gave them something they desperately needed – hope.

Germany had lost the First World War in 1918 and was held responsible for the enormous and expensive reconstruction of Europe. Some German land was taken away and many new restrictions were placed on Germany. The German people were humiliated and wanted a scapegoat for all that had gone wrong. Hitler hated the Jews and all minority groups so he blamed them. He fostered discrimination and resentment, particularly against the Jews. He convinced his followers in the Nazi party and Germans of all ages that they belonged to a superior race, and that Germany should be the leading nation with power over all other countries. He appointed a special group of 'super Nazis' called the SS who made a vow of loyalty and obedience to him, swearing to follow every command, even the order to murder.

'We don't know where this will all lead,' Pappy said sadly. 'Let's hope and pray things will get better.'

Eventually, Mutti and Pappy told us that we would have to sell our home and move into a more affordable apartment. I couldn't imagine leaving our old Victorian house and garden on the corner of my favourite street in my favourite neighbourhood.

'No other place can possibly feel like home,' I said to Heinz.

'I know,' he answered sadly.

I walked through each room slowly to say goodbye. I snapped a picture in my memory of the little table set for tea in my bedroom alcove where I could look out the window across our great city. I stood on the front balcony where Heinz and I spent summer evenings gazing up at the stars. Pappy found me in the dining room which had my favourite red flowers scattered all over the papered walls.

These were walls that had great stories to tell, I thought, *about all of the parties and special holidays we had shared.*

Pappy sensed my sentimental feelings and lifted me up in his arms. 'It will all work out, Evi,' he said. 'We have wonderful memories from all our years here, but we'll make new ones in our new home. And don't forget, we'll be even nearer to Grandmother and Grandfather, and we can visit them as often as we like.'

I felt better, but I could hear a sound in his voice that told me it wasn't easy for him either. At this time I began to learn that disappointments and hardships are a part of life, but families can get through them together.

3.

Confused by an Upside-Down World

My classmates began making comments that confused me. I wondered if this had anything to do with the reports about Germany on the radio, or something they had heard their parents say.

I mentioned it to Heinz: 'I heard one of the boys in my class talking about the Jews today. He called us names I didn't understand, said he didn't want us in the school because we don't belong. Belong where? What does that mean?'

Heinz hesitated before responding. 'He probably wanted to feel important and show that he is better than us. That's what bullies do: they pick on those who are different from themselves and put them down or belittle them. They say mean things that are often not true to convince others to see things their way. It is wrong, Evi, and you must not believe them.'

'I was scared, Heinz. Maybe I shouldn't go back,' I said. I appreciated Heinz's sympathy.

'It is a terrible feeling to be left out,' he added. 'Nobody wants to be left out. But don't pay attention to what the kids are saying. The teachers and parents will help make sure everything is OK.' Heinz put his arm around me and I felt a little better.

Little did we know that soon the entire Jewish population was about to be 'left out', a school child's greatest fear and ultimately history's greatest tragedy.

Adolf Hitler and the Nazis had begun to turn the world upside down. Hitler's idiotic race policy was spreading out of control. Many Germans liked being called 'the master race', believing that they were better and more intelligent than others. They supported Hitler when he passed laws that took away the rights of the Jews which made them 'non-Germans'. They joined in anti-Jewish displays, boycotted Jewish businesses and cheered when Jewish books were burned. Hatred and prejudice grew stronger and stronger. The Nazis put people in prison if they didn't demonstrate support and allegiance to the 'new Germany'. When the prisons got too crowded, they opened slave-labour camps, where large numbers of people were concentrated.

Despite these terrible accounts, many Austrians spoke enthusiastically about Hitler and the Nazis. They wanted to be part of the great German empire and believed Hitler would bring prosperity to our country as well. Then, just two months before my ninth birthday on 13 March 1938, the Nazis marched into Austria. A big parade filled the streets of the capital, Vienna. Thousands of soldiers with hard faces passed by the cheering crowds. Our fellow

Austrians raised their arms with hands facing up in what became known as the Hitler salute.

Most Jewish people, aware of Hitler's atrocities in Germany, stayed at home. Our family gathered at Grandfather Rudolph's house. The adults talked about what they should do, while we children tried to keep ourselves occupied, though we couldn't help but listen to their conversation.

'It can't possibly get so bad in Austria. Our non-Jewish friends won't allow it,' someone said.

'We don't know for sure. Maybe it would be best to leave. But where can we go? Where will it be safe?' Aunt Sylvi answered anxiously.

'We have lived here for our entire lives,' Grandfather said, 'and Austria has been our homeland for generations. We cannot just leave everything and start all over in another country.'

The talking went on until very late that night. Mutti, Pappy, Heinz and I walked home in silence, suspicious of the dark.

'Tomorrow will be a better day,' Mutti said as she kissed us goodnight.

We quickly fell into an exhausted sleep.

The following day was not better. Our community changed overnight. Some acquaintances acted openly hostile to us, as if they were looking at us through different eyes. Many hung the Nazi red, white and black banner with the crooked cross, called a swastika, in front of their homes. They criticized us and made derogatory remarks because we had not shown allegiance to the Nazi party.

I learned that one of my friend's parents didn't want their daughter to play with me any more, as if a nine-year-old girl like me could be dangerous!

Our worst fear came true: Hitler took complete control of the government. All Jews had to have documents for identification with them at all times. People stopped us in the street and told us that we had to show our papers or they would turn us over to the authorities. We couldn't trust anyone.

Jewish men and women who had been proud Austrians, accomplished professionals and active members of society were suddenly faced with the inability to provide shelter, food and safety for their families. Many lost their jobs and businesses, because only Jews would employ them or work for them. Some found a way to escape immediately to Holland, Britain or the United States, but for most people this was next to impossible as it was very difficult to get exit visas to safe countries. It required money, the sacrifice of one's home and possessions, and courage to begin again in a new country among strangers who likely spoke a different language.

Nevertheless, Mutti and Pappy started making arrangements for us. Neither Heinz nor I knew what they were planning, but we took comfort in believing that our parents would keep us safe, no matter what.

The changes in our lives caused great confusion and sadness for everyone. We said 'goodbye' to many of our loved ones. Aunt Sylvi, Uncle Otto and our little cousin, Tom, moved to England. They were very fortunate, since most countries didn't easily grant visas because of the economic depression across Europe and the increasing population of unemployed workers. But Uncle Otto, an expert with a product called Perspex, a forerunner of plastic, managed to convince the proper authorities that his knowledge and experience could be useful to British manufacturing.

Then one of Mutti's cousins also left for England. Her Christian husband had deserted her the day Austria was invaded. She found work as a domestic servant, the only kind of job she could secure that qualified her to receive a visa. Unfortunately, like many other young women, she was treated like a slave and had to work from dawn until dusk, fetching coal early each morning and cleaning the fireplace late at night.

Uncle Ludwig, Aunt Blanca and Gaby were also moving to England. Uncle Ludwig had been working as an art historian for Phaidon Press, a prestigious and successful publisher of art books. His boss was able to arrange for him to set up the company in London. Heinz and I were devastated when Gaby told us.

The Sunday before they left, Heinz, Gaby and I gathered around Uncle Ludwig on the sofa in their living room. He had one of his favourite art books on his lap and, like he had done so many times before, pointed out interesting details in masterpieces of the Greeks, Dutch, Italians and the French to help us learn about the world of art. The paintings were like windows on the stories of those nations.

'This looks like the place we visited last summer,' Heinz said when Uncle Ludwig turned to a picture of a magnificent church with spires touching the sky, towering over a tiny village.

'I wonder if the people who lived there had to worry about their safety, like us,' I said with a sigh.

'I like this one,' Heinz said, pointing to a picture of a girl in a garden of flowers. 'One day I am going to paint a picture just like this of you, Evi, or Mutti, or Gaby, or someone else I know.'

'I think you will be a fine artist, Heinz,' Uncle Ludwig said. 'And your paintings will be in a book for others to see.' Heinz smiled, and I felt proud.

When the time came to say goodbye I wanted to cry. I hated not knowing when or where we would see each other again.

'Chin up,' Pappy said. 'Things always work out eventually.'

Aunt Sylvi had applied for Grandmother and Grandfather to join them in England. It was possible to get permission, but it would take time. I was not anxious for them to leave, but at the same time I wanted them to be safe, too.

Then Pappy came home with news for Mutti, Heinz and me. We finally had a destination, and hope for the future. Pappy had found a large shoe factory in Holland that was going out of business. He shared his innovative ideas with the employers, and convinced them that the changes would make a difference in their success. They happily welcomed him and we were greatly relieved, though I wished secretly that we were moving to England like the rest of our family!

Unfortunately, Pappy could only obtain visitors' visas for us in Holland, so Mutti, Heinz and I could stay with him for just a limited time. Poor Mutti was so upset, thinking she and Pappy had found a solution for our great dilemma, only to be confronted with more problems.

Pappy tried to remain positive. 'The shoe factory is in a little town called Breda in the south of Holland, quite close to the border of Belgium and the capital city of Brussels. Brussels is a large city like Vienna, which will be nice for Mutti,' he said, glancing over at our mother. 'In addition, the Belgians speak French, which everyone but Evi is familiar with. Heinz, this will make it easier for you to continue your studies. And, of course, we can all help Evi learn a new language.'

Though not ideal, it was finally decided: Mutti, Heinz and I would move to Brussels, while Pappy lived in Holland and visited us on the weekends. It all sounded confusing to me. I did not want to move away from our home, our happy memories and our family. For Mutti and Pappy's sake, I tried very hard not to dwell on the changes or fears about the future.

Pappy went on ahead to Holland to begin work. By then it was April 1938, one month after the Nazi invasion. Heinz and I stayed with Mutti while she made final preparations to leave Austria. Each day she sold a few more of our family possessions: the marble-topped table Pappy had been so thrilled to find, the dining-room furniture passed down from Grandfather David. Mutti had to accept whatever little money people offered. Heinz and I felt very sad about it, but she reminded us to keep our spirits up and be thankful for the little things.

Not long after Pappy had begun working in Holland, Heinz arrived home from school with a bloody face. Some of the boys in his class had taunted him and called him names. Then a few grabbed him, hitting and punching. He had a big gash next to his healthy eye. I cried the minute I saw him.

'Why did they do this, Mutti?' he said, the tears streaming down his cheeks.

Heinz couldn't understand such animosity. Mutti was furious. While she carefully tended his wounds, her upsetting and angry words about the vicious attacks on the Jews overflowed like water over a dam. I stood beside Heinz, holding his hand.

'That's it,' Mutti said. 'I'm sending you to Holland now to stay with Pappy. Evi and I will come very soon, after we finish everything here in Vienna.'

Pappy agreed that this was best, and a few days later Mutti and I went with Heinz to the train station. He was twelve years old, which seemed nearly grown up to me. However, as I watched him board the train with groups of strangers, he looked very young. He carried a small suitcase and a satchel stuffed with books. I hated the thought that he would be all alone until he met up with Pappy. I hoped with all my heart that he would arrive safely in Holland. Thank goodness he did!

Mutti didn't let the confusion around us interrupt the tasks that needed attention. We went shopping for clothes and various supplies since we could only take a small sum of money out of Austria. Mutti made sure that all the clothes for Heinz and me had plenty of growing room. As in the past, she made all the decisions about what we would wear. I was not allowed to give my opinion or offer any comment. This didn't bother me until we stopped at Bitman's Department Store.

'We are going to Brussels,' Mutti told the sales assistant, 'and I want a smart coat and hat for my daughter.'

I was aghast when she came out of the storeroom with a bright orange coat and matching Scottish plaid hat.

'That is dreadful,' I announced, almost shouting. 'I am not going to wear that!'

'Of course you will,' said Mutti. 'All the little Belgian girls are wearing smart coats like this.'

She held it up for me to slip my arms inside. I tried to convince her that it was uncomfortable and would never fit. Mutti didn't listen to one thing I said. She went ahead and bought the coat. I was mortified, and decided right then and there that it could sit in the cupboard for all I cared. I was not going to wear an orange coat! In time she dyed it blue and I ended up wearing it a lot!

My concerns paled in comparison to Mutti's. The treatment of Jews in Vienna worsened. In some areas where the more religious Jewish people lived, men were dragged out of their homes and beaten up. Mutti tried to finish a few final details when she heard from Pappy. He insisted that we leave for Holland as soon as possible. Within a few days we were on our way.

Mutti and I arrived safely in Holland to spend a few

weeks with Pappy before moving to Belgium. We were greatly relieved to be away from the Nazis. Only a short time later, in June 1938, many countries around the world refused to take in any more Jewish refugees!

The anxiety of our departure from Vienna disappeared the moment we saw Pappy and Heinz. They ran to greet us and took our few bags in one hand, then wrapped the other arm around our shoulders as we shuffled through the crowds. Pappy led Mutti, and Heinz led me. We talked non-stop the whole way to the house where Pappy had been renting a few rooms.

I told Heinz about everything that had happened. 'Wait until you see all the things Mutti bought for you, Heinz – trousers with extra long legs so you can grow into them and a very smart jacket. But she got a horrible orange coat for me. I'm not going to wear it for anything!' Heinz laughed, and I didn't even let him say one word before I started talking about the train trip.

'There were soldiers on the train, Heinz. They had guns and mean faces. I was so scared. We had to get out of the train several times and show our papers. I had to wear so many extra clothes because Mutti couldn't fit one more thing in the suitcase. I was afraid that my hands would shake and they would notice and suspect that we were smuggling something. Then we would have been sent back, Heinz. It would have been so terrible.

'Well, it is all over now,' Heinz said. 'We are safe here with Pappy.'

Pappy talked about his latest ideas and the success of his business, which was growing rapidly. Mutti smiled and began to relax. It didn't take me long to unwind either.

Breda, the small country town where Pappy lived, was a completely different place from the smart city of Vienna. It was located in the middle of fields of heather. I felt like we were actually on holiday. I wanted to skip and run. I giggled easily as I pulled Heinz alongside me, exploring our new surroundings. He didn't resist, and I guessed that he had missed me. The warmth and friendliness of the Dutch people added to our happiness.

I would have liked to stay in Holland, but Heinz reminded me that we didn't have permission. As our visit came to an end, Pappy talked excitedly about our new life ahead in Brussels and the start of a new school year.

Despite all their worries, Mutti and Pappy acted cheerfully and we didn't notice the deep anxieties they must have felt.

'It is only a short train trip away,' Pappy reassured us. 'And I promise to come every weekend. Evi, you can show me all around, and Heinz, I will love to hear about everything you're learning.'

I found it confusing to move into a new 'home' without Pappy.

'Don't worry, Evi,' Mutti said. 'Things will feel normal as soon as school starts and you are with all the other children your own age.'

'How can Mutti say that things will be normal?' I complained to Heinz. 'We are in a strange place without Pappy. Everyone speaks a language that I cannot understand. I miss home. I miss Austria; my Sunday walks with

Grandfather and hikes in the mountains. I miss my friends, and our aunts, uncles and cousins. I can't picture where everyone has gone or what they are doing. I can't even imagine what baby Tom looks like.'

'We can't do anything about it, Evi, so we might as well think about something else,' Heinz said.

But I heard Mutti talking with Pappy on the telephone about some of the relatives who were missing, and how everyone was worried about Grandmother and Grandfather because they were still in Austria waiting for visas to England. I just couldn't imagine how things were ever going to work out. I tried to cooperate, but I felt discouraged and sad. When I got up each morning I didn't care about what dress Mutti told me to put on, or what plans we had for the day. Nothing seemed to matter. The young girl looking back at me in the mirror was not smiling. She had turned into a poor refugee, with no more parties, no piano lessons for Heinz and no celebrations. Our friends, family and the places and things we loved were far, far away.

It took time and patience for us to get used to our new place. It was small and cramped, with one room for Heinz and me, and the other for Mutti, and Pappy when he came to visit. Our possessions did not fit in the space available, but then most of our things had been sold off. I kept forgetting. I wanted to believe that we had been on holiday and would soon return to our own home, where I had my own room. Sometimes I stood gazing out of the window on to someone else's world. The people in the streets hurried past, as if there were no time for anything but work and important business.

Nevertheless, Mutti encouraged us to be cheerful. She took a photograph of Heinz and me in the garden to send to Pappy. We weren't particularly agreeable. I sat with legs and arms folded, looking a bit cross. Heinz stood protectively behind me, his hands on the back of my chair, glancing down with a sombre expression. When Mutti showed us the printed picture she didn't comment at all about our attitude, but praised us for going along with her positive suggestions.

Little by little, my confusion subsided. The owner of the boarding house where we lived, Madame LeBlanc, had a stepson the same age as me called Jacky. He invited me to play and I found him to be good company. We used a few simple words and gestures, and I realized that we could have fun despite the language barrier. Surprisingly, it wasn't long before I had learned to speak and understand basic French.

However, French at school was an entirely different matter. I felt as if I was lost in a sea of swirling sounds. My classmates were willing to rescue me, but I was completely unhappy. The teacher occasionally turned and looked my way. She gave a little smile, and then spoke something emphatically. Still, I hadn't the slightest idea about what was going on. Many of the lessons involved dialogue back and forth between the teacher and students, everyone chanting answers at the same time. I sat at my desk feeling utterly helpless.

Weeks passed, and it seemed that nothing could break down the wall of misunderstanding. I cried to Mutti in exasperation. Mutti had been a French tutor in Vienna. She decided that perhaps it would help if she gave me regular lessons. But there was so much to learn at once, and she became extremely frustrated with me. Obviously I had added to all her other problems.

'You are such a stubborn child,' Mutti said, when I refused to listen to her explain French verbs. For some reason her method of studying didn't work for me. Mutti was convinced that I simply refused to go about it in the right way.

Why couldn't I have it easy, like Heinz? I thought. *Why does everything have to be so hard?*

All the months of tension and worry built up like a steep mountain, impossible to climb. In my despair I remembered Pappy's encouraging words as we made our way across the sheer passes of the Austrian Alps.

'You'll make it, Evi. Look straight ahead and keep your eyes on the goal and you'll be just fine.'

As we became acquainted with the other people living at Madame LeBlanc's boarding house, I realized that it was a difficult time for everyone. I looked around the large dining room where we ate our meals and noticed Jews from Germany and Austria. Most faced a similar predicament: away from home, from their jobs, friends, families, familiar surroundings, not knowing where to go next.

On some afternoons I went with Mutti to the Centre for Refugees. It was a busy place, and it didn't look very organized with so many people going in and out. But

Mutti reminded me, 'They're doing the best they can.' Pappy would have said the exact same thing.

I sat off to the side while Mutti stood in a couple of different lines. I began to notice the many helpful comments and kind remarks people made to each other. Some of the little children held their mothers' hands tightly, while others were restlessly pushed away. One poor lady had to chase after her son, who darted right out of the building and into the street. She came back to the line looking exhausted.

A few young volunteer workers said '*bonjour*' to me. I responded with the same, and tried to smile appreciatively. I wanted desperately to talk with them, but I just didn't know enough French words. I hoped they didn't think me unfriendly. I hoped they would speak to me next time, when I would be able to say more. As soon as I got home I asked Heinz to help me with French conversation and surprisingly it didn't seem too hard. I much preferred his approach to Mutti's lessons on French grammar.

One day Mutti received a letter from Grandmother Helen and Grandfather Rudolph in Austria. While she read the first few lines of the message her eyes filled with tears and she cried and laughed at the same time. They had received their visas for England.

'Finally!' she sighed. 'Finally they'll be safe! And listen to this, children, they're coming to Brussels to see us first. They should be here in two days!'

I woke early on the morning of their arrival, bursting with excitement and anticipation. Mutti, Heinz and I went

to the Centre for Refugees to meet them. As we wove
through a crowd of people I could feel my heart racing.

'What if something happened on the way?' I thought.
'What if they never make it?'

Suddenly, Heinz spotted Grandfather and hurried to
his side. Our reunion felt absolutely glorious, with
everyone talking, laughing and crying at the same time.

'You have become too thin, Dad. We must fatten you
up while you are here,' Mutti said, trying to speak lightly
but with a choke in her voice.

I could tell it was very hard for her to see her parents
looking anxious and much older. Grandfather kept
nervously glancing over his shoulder. But as we shared
news about some of the good things that were happening,
they felt more at ease.

'Granny, I can't wait till you meet my special friend,
Jacky. He is one of the nicest boys I have ever met. He
reminds me a bit of my friend, Martin. Do you know
what happened to Martin?' I asked, talking so fast that
she didn't have a chance to answer. 'And, Granny, I want
to tell you all about school. Some things are just fine, but
some are not so fine.'

Heinz began asking Grandfather about some of our
family.

'Perhaps we should gather your luggage so we can start
for home, or we are bound to stand here talking all day,'
Mutti said, laughing.

During their brief stay, Heinz told Grandfather about
his studies and how he especially missed playing the piano,
while I shared all my woes with Grandmother. Mutti had

long discussions with them as well, asking advice about everything. She used to see them every day while we lived in Vienna, and desperately missed consulting with Grandmother.

Pappy came to visit us from Holland, and I overheard the grown-ups talking about the Nazis. They said things that frightened me about ghettos in Poland and burning shops and synagogues in Germany. But still I found it hard to imagine the danger. It seemed far away. I couldn't really see how it affected us. After all, we were safe in Brussels. Pappy was nearby in Holland, and I believed it wouldn't be too long before we could live with him there. Meanwhile Grandmother and Grandfather would be settled in England.

Our few days together flew by too quickly, and soon our grandparents had to leave. Their departure brought on another wave of loneliness and longing for the way life used to be. I wished Aunt Sylvi would come walking down the street with Gaby. I wished I could see my friends Kitty and Martin, and all my cousins. I wished we were planning a trip to the mountains. I was miserable with hundreds of wishes floating around in my head. I would have told Heinz all about how I felt, hoping he would have some words of comfort for me, but he had become completely absorbed in his Latin and French homework. Eventually I gave up and went to find Jacky to see if he wanted to play 'dressing up' with a box of old clothes. He agreed and we pretended to be grown-ups in charge of everything.

*

Our problems continued to multiply, but Mutti and Pappy refused to complain. Every time Pappy travelled between Holland and Belgium he had to have approval from the authorities. Officials stamped his passport coming and going, and soon it was filled cover to cover. They treated my distinguished father like a young schoolboy. It seemed that we couldn't do a thing without someone's permission.

'How long are we going to stay in this new place?' I asked Heinz. 'Can't Pappy get a job here? Or why can't we go back to Holland with him and learn Dutch? Hitler and the Nazis are far away, so why do we have to worry about doing all these crazy things?'

Heinz didn't say much. I don't think he knew the answers to my endless questions. He seemed to accept what was happening, as if everything was all right. I talked in circles until I could satisfy myself with a possible solution.

'Pappy will work hard like he always does, and then he will find the perfect place for us and we will all be together again,' I decided.

One day I learned that my good friend Kitty, from Vienna, had come to Brussels with her family. We had been schoolmates and had spent happy times playing together. I couldn't seem to contain my excitement, repeatedly interrupting Heinz's reading to announce my plans to meet Kitty later that day. I felt bad that Heinz didn't have a friend like me to hang around with, but it didn't seem to bother him.

Mutti took a photograph of Kitty and me when she

arrived. We had grown to exactly the same height, and put our arms around each other's shoulders like best friends. We played our favourite games and then lay in front of the fireplace, sharing memories about Austria. In those few wonderful moments the past seemed to come back to life and we pretended that nothing bad had happened at all.

Sophie Yaron

4.

Feeling Renewed

The way of life in Brussels gradually became more familiar, and I started to feel a sense of belonging. In mid December 1938 my school put on a show, giving all of the students an opportunity to demonstrate their progress and the parents a chance to beam with pride. My teacher had given me a long fable by La Fontaine to memorize. It was a story called 'The Ploughman and His Children' that had a moral to be learned about work being a treasure.

I was determined to make an effort and finally prove to everyone, including myself, that I could speak French fluently. Jean de La Fontaine was a French poet. His name meant Jean of the Fountain. I pictured his words like water sprinkling over all the thirsty people. For days before the show, I recited the poem on my walk home from school, then for Mutti and Heinz and as I drifted off to sleep each night.

Finally the evening of my class presentation arrived. My teacher called our names in turn.

'I am happy to introduce a little Austrian Jewish girl who has been working very hard,' she said.

As I walked nervously to the front of the room, my

mind went blank. I closed my eyes for a brief second, straining to find the words floating in my store of memories. When I turned to look at the rows of faces, my knees began to shake, my eyes glazed over and my mouth became dry.

'Come on, Evi, it is your turn now,' my teacher said.

Heinz, sitting to my right under the window, smiled encouragingly at me. In an instant the fable was rolling off my tongue in the beautiful French phrases that told the tale of 'The Ploughman and His Children'. When I came to the end everyone applauded. I looked at Mutti and Heinz. Their faces shone with pride. I felt overjoyed, relieved and extremely pleased with myself.

Once I became part of the class, school was fun. I skipped home at the end of the day to tell Mutti my news. I burst into the room where she was writing letters, tossing my coat and satchel on a chair until I caught her glance and stopped to hang them up. She got us some lemonade and then we sat in a corner of the dining room while I went on and on about all that my classmates had said or done. I had opinions about everything. Sometimes Mutti just listened and nodded as I expounded on my beliefs, interpretations and decisions about the way I thought things should be. At other times she interrupted to express her views and remind me to make good decisions so I would be able to look forward to a good future.

I found new friends at school and new friends at home. An elderly refugee couple, also living in the boarding house, took a liking to Heinz and me. We adopted them as our great-aunt and -uncle. They often gave us treats; my favourite was a famous Belgian chocolate called Côte d'Or, which means 'Gold Coast'. As they placed it in my hands, my mouth began to water and I felt anxiousness well up inside me. Not only was the chocolate delicious but each package contained a special treasure: a picture postcard of the royal family of Belgium. This was the most important part for me.

'Oh, thank you,' I cried with a quick hug for each of them.

They watched me slowly fold back the wrapping to find a photograph of Queen Astrid, King Leopold III, their two handsome sons and one daughter. Their names were exquisite: Prince Baudouin Albert Charles Leopold Axel Marie Gustave, Prince Albert Félix Humbert Théodore Christian Eugène Marie and Princess Joséphine-Charlotte Ingeborg Elisabeth Marie-José Marguerite Astrid. Sometimes I closed my eyes and imagined that our world was perfect like theirs.

I collected these postcards like all my friends did, and we were constantly swapping them. I became fanatical about it, and considered the pictures my most precious possessions. Heinz was able to get a lot of them for me from his friends because they thought it was childish to have such a collection. He turned this into a business venture. As soon as he acquired three pictures, he would make me do a job to earn them, like clean his shoes or organize his books. I felt like his servant, but it was definitely worth it.

Early that spring 'Auntie' and 'Uncle' bought us a kite

and took us kite-flying at the Belgian seaside. Heinz carefully unwrapped the packaging, measured the string precisely and then tied it patiently. I could hardly contain my excitement. Finally he handed it to me with a look of pride on his face.

'You must keep the tail from getting snagged by anything on the ground,' he instructed me.

I reached up, stretching my arms as far as I could, then, holding the string securely, I ran. Within seconds something invisible pulled on the kite and took it away.

'Look, look,' I shouted joyfully as the wind carried it high into the air where it could fly freely. How I wished I could fly like a kite, away from all the troubles and worries of the world.

In the meantime, Mutti worried about the danger of our position as stateless refugees. I heard her talking with another mother from Austria about how we had no rights, no state to help us in any way. She also worried about our separation from Pappy. He tried to come every weekend, but sometimes it was impossible. Mutti knew it was hard for us to be without our father. We longed for his goodnight hugs, his words of reassurance and the security of having him near.

Mutti also missed being in charge of her own home and the companionship of Aunt Sylvi and Aunt Blanca. Her friends at the Centre for Refugees couldn't begin to provide the comfort and closeness of family.

One day Mutti received a letter in the post from her sister and parents in England. Everyone was well.

Grandmother was happily taking care of Tommy each day while Aunt Sylvi and Uncle Otto went to work. At first Grandfather had been at a loss, refusing to learn any English. But one evening he went to the local pub where he sat down to play the piano. The regular patrons and servicemen and -women loved hearing him play and he soon became the most popular entertainer in their town. Mutti read the letter to Heinz and me, smiling and tearful at the same time.

Heinz excelled at his school work, grew in popularity among his classmates and continued studies in a number of languages. He asked me to test him on his vocabulary, though I didn't have a clue what he was saying. I just liked the funny sounds of the words, a bit like scribbles on a piece of paper where the lines and colours make patterns but no one can figure out what the artist has drawn.

As my tenth birthday approached in May 1939, I made up my mind that I should have a party.

'Oh, please, Mutti,' I nagged. 'I would love to have a party with ten candles on the cake.'

She finally agreed after seeking approval from Madame LeBlanc. To my great delight, Madame even offered to make the cake!

I eagerly wrote the invitations to hand out to three special friends in my class. At break time they asked me what presents I would like, and we giggled as we decided together what games we would play. The following morning I ran up to each of them, one at a time, anxious to share a few more exciting ideas. All three told me that their parents wouldn't allow them to come. I couldn't believe it. I felt bewildered, hurt, like an outcast.

Why can't they come? I thought. *Did I do something wrong?*

I started to cry many times that day. Then I told Heinz and Mutti when I got home from school.

'It's because we're Jewish,' Heinz said. 'They aren't true friends, Evi, if they turned on you like that.'

By then terrible things were happening to the Jews in Germany and Austria. Hitler's propaganda had spread to other European countries, including Belgium, and people began to fear being seen with Jews. They believed we were dangerous, even the children!

Mutti tried to make me feel better. 'Friends will come and go, Evi, but you will always have your family,' she said, giving me a big hug.

The hurtfulness caused by my friends vanished when Mutti announced that my biggest birthday wish was about to come true. She and Pappy had made plans for a family holiday. It wouldn't take place until late in the summer, but it gave us something to look forward to.

We travelled to a seaside resort called Zandvoort, about an hour from Amsterdam. The weather was warm and sunny. We spent two carefree weeks playing hide and seek in and out of the sand dunes, swimming and taking long walks at the water's edge. The days were utterly blissful and Heinz and I didn't exchange one word about the danger of the previous months. Mutti and Pappy must have been happy too, because they joined right in the fun, never mentioning the gravity of their concerns.

Pappy hired bikes for all four of us. We laughed together about Mutti's awkwardness with vehicles. The first time she had driven a car, she careened right into a tree. Even a bicycle was a bit hazardous for her. Heinz stayed behind with Mutti, patiently waiting for her to catch up, while Pappy and I sped across the flatlands. I liked to pedal as fast as my legs could go, and then stand up and glide.

We stopped to rest in the grassy sand dunes. They were so high that we could each lie down just a few feet apart from each other and completely disappear from sight. Unfortunately, Mutti lost one of her rings, a treasured keepsake.

'Oh, Erich, what shall I do? We were all having such a lovely time, and now I've gone and spoiled it,' she said.

'Don't worry, Mutti, Evi will find it for you,' Pappy consoled her.

I had excellent vision and Pappy suspected I might like the challenge, but finding anything in all that sand seemed absolutely impossible. Nevertheless, I tried looking just to satisfy Mutti. To everyone's great surprise, I found the ring. Heinz teased me repeatedly after that.

'Don't worry about losing anything,' he said, 'Eagle-eyes-Evi will always be able to find it.'

Everything seemed to improve during that time. We actually believed that things would get better for us. But then we had to return to Brussels and to school.

At the beginning of September 1939 I learned that my apprehension about school was nothing compared to the enormity of world events. The Germans had already invaded Czechoslovakia and signed a 'Pact of Steel' with Italy. Then they invaded Poland. Leaders of France, England, Australia and New Zealand announced that Hitler's campaign for supremacy could no longer be tolerated. They declared war on Germany and the Second World War began. Canada also declared war on Germany a few days later, joining the group of countries called the Allies.

We could sense the tension increasing for everyone. No one knew what would happen next. Even Pappy became restless. Restrictions on travel between countries became very tight. Fearing that the border between Holland and Belgium could close, Pappy tried to speed up the arrangements for us to live with him in Amsterdam.

When I shared my excitement with Mutti about being reunited with Pappy she seemed anxious and upset. I couldn't begin to imagine all that was on her mind. We were refugees, and I didn't realize how difficult it would be for us to relocate. In the end it took six long months of waiting for visas, anticipating a reunion with Pappy, worrying that things would get worse, hoping for the best.

Our spirits were renewed when we finally arrived in Amsterdam in February 1940. There was a welcoming atmosphere that felt safe because Holland had remained a neutral country during the First World War, and generally people felt it would stay neutral again. Everyone shared the same sense of security.

Pappy met us at the train station where we laughed happily to see each other. He told us excitedly about the lovely apartment he had found for us, the countless boats on the canals and the wooden bridges.

'You can look through the planks to the water below, Evi, and watch the boats pass by,' he said, knowing how much I would enjoy this.

We rode on the tram past shops, cafes and along the River Amstel. Pappy reminded Mutti that our rented furnished apartment was only a short ride from the city centre, a place that she would enjoy visiting. I recited the address to Heinz: 46 Merwedeplein. Our neighbourhood was easy to find, since it was near the only skyscraper in the city, twelve storeys tall. Our apartment building was new, bright and inviting, with an open space in the middle where children could play. I immediately ran across the grass, doing cartwheels until Heinz called for me to stop.

'Come on, Evi. Let's go inside,' he said eagerly.

Pappy led us up some stairs to a covered hallway with six doors, three on either side leading to apartments on the first, second and third floors. Ours was in the middle. When we stepped inside our new home Mutti immediately spotted the baby grand piano in the front room.

'Oh, Erich,' she cried. She sat down at once and played a familiar piece by Johann Strauss that brought back memories of Austria. She beamed with happiness and displayed a peaceful look we had not seen for a long time. Pappy showed us all around our new home. Each little detail seemed so wonderful and special.

When we entered the kitchen he looked at Mutti and

said, 'Fritzi, I believe cooking will be a new venture for you.'

'It will be a pleasure,' she said with a smile, 'as long as everyone can exercise patience while I learn.'

Within days Mutti found a piano teacher for Heinz. He spent hours practising his exercises over and over until I was ready to beg him to stop. Then he played around with jazz tunes and, once in a while, if I was very lucky, my favourite Yiddish folksong.

He sat straight and tall on the piano stool, turning to catch my eye as his fingers began the familiar, '*Bei mir bist du sheyn.*'

'It means, "when you are with me, you are beautiful"!' he announced.

I jumped up after the first couple of notes and began twirling and hopping about the room. I felt like a famous performer bringing a story to life for an adoring audience. Mutti and Pappy applauded, thrilled to see us laughing and carefree.

Mutti noticed how much I had grown and suggested that we should shop for some new clothes, something we had not done for nearly two years. Pappy teased Heinz about his rapid growth.

'Soon you'll tower above me,' he said. 'Here, Evi and Heinz, let's mark your height on the wall. Then we can keep track of your growth.'

I went first. He placed a book above my head, gently touching my hair, and then asked if I was standing tall. Mutti stood off to the side with a look of contentment.

'Now you have made your marks here,' he said, drawing a pencil line, 'so this room is truly yours.'

Only one month later, Pappy had to make a higher line for both of us.

Despite the progression of the war, everyone continued to believe that Holland was safe from the Nazi invasion across Europe. Nevertheless, we practised drills with all our neighbours in case there was an air raid. People gathered outside in the streets with cheerful greetings, asking after each other's health and giving help and advice where needed.

Pappy's good friend, Martin Rosenbaum, and his wife, Rosi, especially liked Heinz and me. They were unable to have children of their own, and frequently complimented us on our good behaviour and active curiosity.

'They are delightful, Erich,' Mr Rosenbaum said with a longing in his eyes.

We loved the attention and showered our affection on them.

Heinz and I knew we had much to be thankful for. We echoed our parents' hopeful remarks, telling each other that everything was going to work out. We realized that there were many people who cared about us, like the Rosenbaums and all of our relatives. And despite all the changes, our family had managed to stay safe. After all, we had made it to Holland and we were all back together again.

Heinz and I talked about this during late-night chats

on the balcony outside our bedroom. On warm nights when there was no rain, one of us would whisper to the other, 'Looks like a perfect night for a midnight feast.' I looked forward to this special time with Heinz. I felt like I was almost on the same level as him, like I had grown closer to his age.

I prepared a plate of stolen goodies from the icebox on the balcony. I piled on the sausage and cheese, surprised that it never looked like any food was missing the next day. Heinz tiptoed around the room collecting blankets and pillows. Then we huddled in our little space under the stars, munching, whispering, giggling and dreaming about a happy future when the war would be over. The window to Mutti and Pappy's bedroom was only a few feet away from the balcony. They must have known what we were up to, but they never said a word about it.

5.

Included in a Circle of Friends

We had a brief respite from school due to our move, and when the time came to return I worried again about fitting in and making friends. I wasn't like Heinz, whose special talents made him popular with everyone. I was keen on working with my hands, and Pappy often let me fix things around the apartment. But I struggled with schoolwork, and didn't really like new situations in which I felt awkward and incompetent.

Heinz seemed to adapt effortlessly to change, dealing with his feelings through his artwork or his music. Mutti told me that writing helped her to cope with frustrations and worries; it helped her put things in perspective. She also formed a music ensemble, playing piano with two string musicians, which served as a wonderful diversion to all the uncertainties.

My feelings, on the contrary, were right on the surface. I was miserable and anxious about school and everyone knew it. I complained about having to learn another language, this time Dutch. Mutti reminded me that most of the students in Holland were learning French, in which I spoke fluently by then.

As it turned out, my teacher spoke French as a second language. I became a bit too confident and bold in class and when she mispronounced her French words I corrected her, the way Mutti had corrected me. My teacher felt humiliated and took out her anger on me, displaying spiteful looks and muttering unkind comments. It didn't bother me one bit. Instead, I felt as if I had accomplished something noteworthy and was pleased to see that it made me quite popular with my classmates.

On the other hand, it took me longer to make friends on the square outside our apartment. If Heinz had come out with me it would have been much easier, because he was much more approachable than me. I didn't like how the children who had lived there for years formed cliques and left others out.

To my great relief, some of my classmates from school showed up and saved the day. They asked me to join them, and we played for hours: first marbles, then hopscotch and then skipping. During large group games like rounders, everyone recognized my agility and speed. From then on, when sides were chosen I always got picked first. Gradually I felt more confident and found it easier to join in.

I also received quite a bit of attention and cheering when I did my gymnastics. There was an iron railing alongside the buildings between the entrance doors. I loved to hang off the railing, with my arms supporting my upper torso and feet extended out. Mutti's cousin Litty, who had coached me in gymnastics, would have been so proud.

I forgot about all our troubles when we were having so much fun. If given a chance, I would have played with my friends until the night became pitch-black. Each day after school I ran out to join them, not wanting to miss out on anything. But Mutti and Pappy always made sure I did my homework, helped with the chores and sat down for supper on time. At first, when Pappy called me to come in, I moaned and complained it wasn't fair, but eventually I gave in with a pout on my face and a 'house arrest' for my stubbornness.

Although Heinz was too busy with his studies to join in my activities, he liked to hear all about my escapades. I loved my new black bike, which I rode through the streets of Amsterdam and across the canals, looking as if I had lived there all my life.

One day Pappy had a surprise for Heinz. With so many lakes in Holland, sailing was very popular. Pappy had noticed Heinz's special interest in sailing after we went on a weekend outing with some friends who had a boat. Heinz would sit on the bow with his guitar, serenading us for hours, even at risk of sunburn. So Pappy found a small sailing boat that Heinz would be able to manage himself. Pappy nearly burst with pride watching Heinz hoist the sail for the first time. As Heinz stood proudly for a photograph, I waited on shore for permission to come aboard.

'Welcome aboard, Miss,' Heinz said, trying to sound official. 'We will be sailing at 0900 hours; the winds are moderate southwesterly. I am your captain, so you need not worry about anything.'

I sat in Heinz's little boat and looked up at my big brother, his hand on the sail, his beaming face outlined by a bright blue sky; I would have sailed with him anywhere!

Every once in a while I took a break from my friends to listen to Heinz play the piano. He had collected sheet music for all the popular songs and could easily play just about anything. I stretched out on the floor at the foot of the piano while he introduced me to the interesting rhythms and jazzy melodies of an American composer, named George Gershwin. His composition, 'Rhapsody in Blue', became Heinz's favourite. He loved playing it, and I loved hearing it, over and over again.

Heinz started a band with some friends, playing guitar and accordion. On warm spring afternoons the group would perform outside. All the local children would come to listen. I greatly enjoyed seeing a crowd gather round, unfolding blankets to sit on the grass and gaze up admiringly at my brother, the band leader. I wanted everyone to know that I was Heinz's sister.

One of Heinz's friends was a boy named Herman, who liked me very much. He asked Heinz to tell me that he wanted me to be his girlfriend. I had no interest at all, and thought Herman was far too clever for me. One day Heinz found me in my bedroom and announced that Herman had come to see me. He stood directly behind Heinz, while I sat on my bed, determined to send him away. Then he stepped forward and shyly stretched out his hand to give me some flowers. His face turned very red as he asked if I would please become his girlfriend.

My embarrassment and sympathy for him rose to the surface, and I said yes. But from then on whenever he came to see me, I always sent Heinz to tell him that I was not in. Eventually he got the message.

In time I began to make special friends. I especially liked Suzanne Lederman, who was in my class and liked the same kind of fun and excitement as me. I admired her bright violet eyes and her long bouncy plaits. Suzanne's apartment building was behind ours. I could look from my bedroom window across the small back gardens to her room on the third floor. We worked out a secret code and sent messages to one another.

Suzanne often played with a lively and popular girl, named Anne Frank, who also lived on our square. Sanne (Suzanne), Anne and a third friend, nicknamed Hanne, would sit together looking at fashion magazines and pictures of film stars. They also giggled over boys, a very silly activity in my estimation. I had a brother, so a boy was nothing special for me.

Sometimes the parents of our peers went out of their way to make us feel accepted. Anne Frank had invited me over to her apartment which was opposite ours in the same square on the Merwedeplein. Her father greeted me with kindness and warmth, and I realized where Anne got her friendly qualities from. When Mr Frank detected my discomfort with the Dutch language, he made a point of talking to me in German.

The Franks had a large cat that purred softly when I picked it up. I cradled him like a baby, longing for a pet of my own. I tickled him under his neck and he closed his eyes with pure contentment. I even talked to him as if he could understand. I noticed Mr Frank out of the corner of my eye, watching me with an amused look. He was much older than Pappy and reminded me a little of Grandfather Rudolph. Eventually, Mrs Frank called Anne and me into the kitchen for lemonade. She sat at the table with us and listened to our happy chatter – sounding like carefree children without a problem in the world.

Later that evening, I sat at my bedroom window watching the night descend. I thought about our new friends, our lovely home and something that Pappy often said: 'the good always outweighs the bad'. While I greatly missed all of our extended family and the splendour of Vienna, I loved being in Amsterdam.

6.

Hidden from Danger

The world was becoming an increasingly dangerous place. In April 1940 Germany invaded Denmark and Norway. Even when Heinz and I talked about this news, we calculated that there weren't enough Nazis to invade every country in Europe. And everyone still believed that Holland would be left out of the war.

Meanwhile, I was worried about more personal concerns. Some time during the move to Holland my picture-card collection of the royal family from the Belgian 'Gold Coast' chocolate was lost. I reacted to this discovery with heart-breaking anguish. Then I learned that even the royal children had sorrows. Their mother died in a car accident when the family was on holiday in the Swiss Alps. The king and queen had taken a drive along winding roads with sharp turns. The car went out of control over a cliff, and the queen was killed. I shuddered to think of what it must have been like for the children when they received the devastating news. Somehow losing my precious collection didn't seem quite so terrible.

One day I found a little kitten near our apartment. She fitted perfectly in the cupped bowl that I made with my hands. I lifted her nose up to mine, and laughed as she tickled me with her delicate movements.

'You have a new family now,' I told her, completely sure that I could convince Mutti to let her stay.

Pappy's face lit up as he watched Heinz and me with our new pet. He glanced at Mutti and signalled his approval, and reluctantly Mutti let us keep her.

One day our little kitten just disappeared. It happened out of the blue. There seemed no way to anticipate or prevent it. We searched absolutely everywhere and couldn't find her. My world collapsed. While I cried inconsolably, everyone else's world was about to be turned upside down, too.

Late in the night on 10 May 1940, the day before my eleventh birthday, we heard airplanes overhead. Pappy turned on the radio. German troops were parachuting into Holland, blowing up bridges and marching across the border. Everyone was stunned. The Dutch had prevented the Germans from invading during the First World War by opening the dykes and flooding the country, but progress had changed the face of warfare. Fighter planes were dropping bombs and soldiers inside the borders.

The Nazis also invaded France, Belgium and Luxembourg on the very same day. Then, on 14 May they bombed Rotterdam, the second biggest city in Holland, killing more than one thousand civilians. The Dutch army fought bravely, but had no chance against such an overpowering force. The royal family fled to England, and Holland surrendered.

Thousands of Jews hurried to the coast, hoping to

escape on one of the ships in port. People were frantic, for many of them, like us, had already left other countries because of the Nazi terror. We gathered a few belongings with the same intent, but too many people were trying to leave at once. We didn't have a chance. After several anxious hours we turned around and walked slowly home, hand in hand, without exchanging a single word.

Within the first few weeks of occupation the Nazis ordered all the Jews in Holland to move to Amsterdam. Pappy could no longer travel to his shoe factory in Brabant. Like so many others, he was again without a job.

What is everyone supposed to do? I thought. *Where will Pappy get money for food and the things we need? How long can this go on?*

Fortunately, Pappy was always resourceful. He had ideas about selling handbags that could be made at home. For a time this helped take care of our needs, along with those of many others whom he employed.

Initially the danger of the Nazi occupation didn't seem too threatening. But they were very clever. They imposed restrictions on the Jews gradually, at first merely requiring that we stay with our own kind, shopping only at Jewish shops. Then we weren't allowed in cinemas and public places like swimming pools, which made life quite difficult, but still tolerable.

As children, we didn't take our predicament too seriously until it became clear that Mutti and Pappy were frightened. They had begun hearing terrifying stories about death camps. They sat at the kitchen table, drinking cup after cup of tea and deliberating about their plans for our family. I wanted desperately to help find a solution, but knew it was best not to interrupt.

Meanwhile, Heinz and I shared our own fears.

'Do you think Pappy will have to leave us again to find a job?' I asked. 'Mutti said the work he is doing can't last for long. What if he goes all the way to America and there is no possibility for us to go with him? That's so far away, and maybe we won't be able to find him.'

For once, my brother couldn't find a way to reassure me. 'I don't know, Evi. I don't even know if Pappy can really keep us safe any more. Some Jews are being taken away. The Nazis could come for us, too. I'm really scared, Evi. I'm really afraid of dying . . .' he said softly.

I didn't know what to say, so I hugged him and suggested we talk to Pappy.

The following evening, when we were all together, Heinz said, 'Pappy, what will happen to us if we die? Will we just disappear?'

Pappy glanced at Mutti, looked at me and then turned to Heinz with sad eyes.

He spoke slowly and thoughtfully. 'We are part of a long chain of people. You and I are each one of the links. So are Evi, Mutti, your grandparents, aunts, uncles, cousins and all the people we know and love, even those we don't know. Every link is important. When you have children you will live on through them.'

'But what if we don't have any children?' Heinz interrupted.

Pappy patted the sofa, inviting us to sit on either side

of him. He opened his arms and wrapped them around Heinz and me while he continued, pausing between his thoughts as if he were looking to some distant realm for the answers.

'Children, I promise you this: everything you do leaves something behind; nothing gets lost. All the good you have accomplished will continue in the lives of the people you have touched. It will make a difference to someone, somewhere, sometime, and your achievements will be carried on. Everything is connected, like a chain that cannot be broken.'

On that dark night Mutti and Pappy cast an unforgettable impression on my mind and heart. While I didn't really understand Pappy's words, I remembered them many times during the months and years that followed. I found strength and reassurance in his promise. Though I never talked to Heinz about it again, I felt certain that he did, too.

Pappy listened religiously to the news broadcasts from Great Britain about the defeat of the Allied armies. Then in August 1940 the reports became even more devastating. The Germans were bombing airfields and factories in England. By September they had conducted massive air raids on the cities of London, Southampton, Bristol, Cardiff, Liverpool and Manchester. Mutti worried desperately about all of our family in England.

The danger around us increased as well. By then the Nazis were everywhere. Everything about them generated 'fear': the way they looked, their actions, their voices and their gestures. They watched us with glaring eyes and said cruel and threatening words as we walked past. They posted signs with lists of restrictions and orders: Jews are not allowed to take the tram or the train. Jews are not permitted to walk on the pavement, sit in the park, take photographs or visit the zoo. Jews cannot go to certain shops, restaurants, libraries or concert halls. Jews have to be home by 8 p.m.

The Nazis took away our bicycles and Heinz's sailing boat. Mutti and Pappy helped us deal with each disappointment, one at a time. Then we had to hand over our radios and Pappy got very upset. He could no longer listen to the British broadcasts which reported the progress of the Allied army, and Mutti and Heinz would greatly miss hearing the performances of the London Philharmonic.

We were becoming terribly disheartened. Many of our Jewish friends had been rounded up and taken away to unknown destinations, and escape seemed impossible. The Nazi empire had spread as far as Romania, North Africa, Yugoslavia and Greece. Japan joined in an agreement with Italy and Germany, and the three nations, called the Axis powers, threatened to take over the whole world. It was like a bad dream, only we couldn't wake up.

Heinz helped all of us to briefly forget our grave dilemma when he played the piano. I sat spellbound watching his hands fly freely across the keys as he played the classical works of Frederic Chopin, Franz Schubert and sometimes his favourite, George Gershwin. When he stopped, Mutti often asked him to play just a little while longer.

Mutti, Pappy and Heinz surprised me with a special celebration for my twelfth birthday. Mutti made a cake with ingredients she had been saving for quite some time, since food rationing made it hard to get sugar, eggs, milk, chocolate and lard. Pappy wrote verses in a card about how proud he was of me. Heinz gave me one of his favourite books, Mark Twain's *The Adventures of Huckleberry Finn*. He also played 'happy birthday' to me on the piano while everyone sang.

Then Heinz asked if I wanted to play Monopoly, which surprised me since he didn't usually play. My friends and I were fanatical about the game. They came over after lunch almost every day so that we could play before returning to school for the afternoon. We never had time to finish, so we left the game out, only to find that the kitten had overturned it. So Heinz made a little table where we could leave it safely.

'At least the kitten can't upset your game any more, now that he is gone,' Heinz said as I finished eating my birthday cake.

This was a sad reminder. Even with all the wonderful birthday wishes, it was hard to be happy for long. I cried when I learned that Jews weren't allowed to go to the cinema. I wanted desperately to see Walt Disney's new film, *Snow White and the Seven Dwarfs*. After supper one night Heinz began unpacking some large pieces of cardboard and got out his crayons.

'Come here, Evi,' Heinz said. 'I have something to show you.'

He beckoned me to sit on the carpet in front of our

large picture windows. Then he placed the cardboard in the window casings. Mutti told me that everyone needed to black out their apartment lights at night in case there was an air raid.

'Most people have black paper blinds,' she explained, 'but Heinz decided to buy cardboard so he could do something special just for you.'

I watched intently as Heinz drew seven little characters and the beautiful Snow White on our blackout coverings. As the figures came to life with his lines and colours, he told the whole story. This meant more to me than going to see the film at the cinema.

The Jews were not the only ones in danger. The Nazis deported and imprisoned political opponents. Communists in particular, along with gypsies, Jehovah's Witnesses, the mentally handicapped and the disabled were all at risk of imprisonment and deportation. Hitler and the Nazis believed they were all subhuman and wanted to get rid of them. Hitler wanted a superior race of perfect men and women to make Germany great again. I couldn't imagine how the Germans dared to believe that they were better than everyone else.

In September Heinz attended a Jewish school, and I joined ten children who were my age for lessons at a Jewish teacher's home. When my classmates and I finished our first course of studies, all the students decided that we would give our teacher a token of our appreciation. We chose two budgies in a cage, which I kept for one week until it was time to present our gift. Meanwhile, all the children came to our apartment every day to feed the birds and play with them.

One morning I woke to discover that one of the birds was dead in the cage. It lay there perfectly frozen, with feathers still soft and pretty. I believed for a moment that if I wished hard enough it would move again. But no such magic existed.

I was desperately afraid to tell my classmates about this tragedy. Mutti promised she would get another bird that day, but the one she brought home looked quite different. Eventually, I had to own up and admit the truth to everyone. The children were surprisingly agreeable, and no one seemed upset. However, I couldn't forget about the bird that had died.

I returned home from my teacher's apartment one afternoon and found Mutti sewing patches on all our coats and jackets. The Nazis had decreed that every Jewish person must wear the Jewish Star of David on their clothing at all times. If they were stopped without it they would be immediately arrested. When Mutti said that we would have to be absolutely sure that the Star of David was always visible on our clothing, I burst out with a string of complaints. My anger and frustration had reached their peak; I didn't even hear all the words that poured out of my mouth.

'We are like outcasts!' I shouted finally.

Mutti lifted her head and looked straight at me. The sight of her tears stopped my flow of angry words. 'Never take off your coat if your dress doesn't have a star on it,' she warned, her voice shaking.

I put my arms around Mutti's shoulders and kissed her wet cheek. I wanted her to know I would do what she said.

A large group of Dutch workers joined together in protest against the injustices towards the Jews and refused to report for work. All the trains and trams in Amsterdam were brought to a halt for two whole days. The Nazis were furious and threatened to make arrests if work didn't resume immediately. Still, the Dutch found ways to fight back. Some brave Christians put the yellow Star of David on their clothing to confuse the Nazis and show their compassion for the Jews. The Dutch Resistance blew up bridges, destroyed Nazi supplies, attacked patrols and formed a communication network to help the Jews. Many lost their lives. We were deeply appreciative of their courage, kindness and sacrifice!

The Nazis began rounding up Jewish men and teenage boys, supposedly sending them off to work in labour camps to help Germany with the war effort. Their families left behind never knew what happened. In fact, most were taken to concentration camps, then on to death camps. The Germans had built hundreds of these camps in Germany, Poland and Austria. The British news had broadcast warnings on the radio that the Jews were being systematically killed, but people didn't want to believe it.

Pappy found out that the safest place to hide was in the hospital. So he contacted a doctor he knew who worked in a hospital and arranged to have Heinz admitted on the pretext that he needed to have medical testing. In the midst of this crisis, Heinz again found a creative outlet. He wrote poetry during his hospital stay.

The Hospital

A long day in the hospital
Is lots of fun for me
Although our ward is almost full
It's the very best place to be.

There's Mr Hillesum in the bed nearby
A very friendly old man
You can often find him on the pot
Which he likes to use when he can.

The nurses are all just fine
You can simply take your pick
The hospital is a fun place to be
Especially when you're not feeling sick.

If you're not really ill, then come to our ward
It's great for a vacation
And as I'm on holiday, I believe
I'm in a lucky location.

(freely translated from the Dutch)

It wasn't long before Pappy brought Heinz home. Some hospitals were being raided as well. The Nazis were taking

Jewish patients right out of their beds and deporting them to the concentrations camps.

One day I saw a man being arrested. He looked like he was Pappy's age. The Nazi soldier was hitting him and shouting and pushing him into a truck. A sick feeling welled up inside me. I thought surely I would cry or scream or be unable to move from the spot, transfixed at the horror. But fear kept my legs moving, and I hurried past. Countless incidents like this were taking place in Amsterdam and in cities all across Europe, and it got to the point where the Jews had no safe haven.

Food was becoming scarce and so Pappy decided that we should set aside supplies each week in case a time came when we didn't have enough to eat. This was a difficult task because all food was rationed and already we could only get small amounts of the things we needed. Nonetheless, we took regular trips to carry whatever we could to the warehouse Pappy had rented for storage.

'You have prepared well,' Pappy said proudly as he looked at the provisions Mutti set on the kitchen table.

He made four piles, one for each of us to pack. My satchel was so full I could hardly close it. Somehow I managed with the bag, but my heart was heavy. Everything that was happening felt heavy. The sun shone brightly on that lovely afternoon and I couldn't help feeling how wrong and unfair life was. When we crossed over the canal I could see reflections in the water. We used to see interesting patterns of buildings and bike-riders in the ripples, but now every movement was threatening and menacing.

Mutti, Heinz and me, Vienna, 1930

My father, Erich,
diving into an
ice-cold lake, 1936

My friend Kitty from
Vienna, and me on the
Belgian coast, 1939

Paßstelle der Deutschen Botschaft
Brüssel
(Ausstellende Behörde)

Brüssel, den -4.12.39. 193

Kinderausweis Nr. 3926

(Nur gültig bis zur Vollendung
des fünfzehnten Lebensjahrs)

Familienname: Geiringer

Rufname: Heinz

Geboren am 12. Juli 1926

Staatsangehörigkeit: Deutsch

Wohnsitz (dauernder Aufenthalt):

Brüssel

A 56 (6. 32) Reichsdruckerei, Berlin

Heinz's identity card. His nationality was given as
German, although he was Austrian.

Heinz and me in
Brussels, 1939.
Heinz was very
proud of his new
bicycle.

Heinz (13), Jacky (8) and
me (10) in the garden
at the boarding house
in Brussels, 1939

my parents in
Zandvoort, a Dutch
seaside town, in
1940

Mutti, Heinz and me in
Amsterdam, 1940

The Merwedeplein, Amsterdam. All the
children played in the square.

These are the last two photos of Heinz and me before
we went into hiding in 1942.

Holland, 1948
(I was still able
to walk on my hands!)

Grandfather Rudolf at the piano in
a pub in Darwin, Lancashire, 1943

Some of Heinz's paintings

How did we get to this point where we have to worry about hiding food? What happened to our happy family and happy home? Why do the problems of the world have to interfere with our lives? Why do we have to be afraid?

I had all these thoughts tumbling around in my head as we swiftly entered the warehouse. I held my breath and prayed that no one saw what we were doing. We flew up two flights of stairs, Pappy unlocked the door and we rushed inside. I set the heavy satchel down and sighed with relief!

'Put the tins of tomatoes in the suitcase with the olive oil and rice,' Pappy instructed us efficiently, 'and the sardines and chocolate over here.'

'Shall I put the condensed milk with the cocoa?' I said, wanting to be helpful.

'That's a good idea,' Mutti said. 'Thank you, Evi, thank you, Heinz. You have been so good about pitching in. One day we will be glad we went to all this trouble.'

Pappy did everything possible to avoid danger and keep our family from being arrested. He obtained information from other Jews and the Dutch Resistance. Through them he had learned how the Nazis had murdered more than 30,000 Jews at Kiev in the Ukraine. He heard that on 7 December, the Japanese bombed the US naval base at Pearl Harbor, and America entered the war. Then Germany, an ally of Japan, declared war on the United States. British Prime Minister Winston Churchill and US President Franklin Roosevelt had a major task before them.

One night in spring 1942 Pappy called Heinz and me

to the kitchen table. Mutti had set a pot of tea out and poured a cup for everyone as Pappy began to talk.

'I am trying very hard to protect us,' he said with great seriousness, 'but you know that the terrible danger of the Nazis is all around us now and they are determined to find all the Jews living in Amsterdam and send them away. Still, there are wonderful people who are giving up their own safety to help us. Right now they are working to find places for us to hide.'

We had suspected that other Jewish families had gone into hiding, but didn't want to think about this possibility for ourselves.

'What do you mean by "places"?' Heinz said.

'Unfortunately it is too risky for all four of us to hide in the same place. Our chances of survival will be greater if Heinz stays with me, and Evi stays in a different place with Mutti.'

Survival! I thought. *Was Pappy saying that one of us might die?*

In that instant I could no longer follow his words. I had so many confusing thoughts in my head, that nothing made any sense. I just stared at Pappy until he indicated that it was time to say goodnight, then went to bed in a daze.

The idea of splitting us up must have been excruciating for Pappy and Mutti. It certainly was for me! Pappy and Heinz had protected Mutti and me. We needed them. But, once again, our parents chose not to surrender the burden of our situation. Instead, they busied themselves with preparations.

Pappy contacted someone in the Dutch Resistance who helped him get false identity papers, in case the Nazis stopped us or we had to move to different hiding places. Mutti was to become Mefrouw Bep Ackerman, and I was her daughter, Jopie Ackerman. I couldn't get used to the strange idea of becoming someone else. I kept on forgetting when and where I was born. Heinz, on the other hand, didn't have any problem remembering all the important information, and he didn't argue about everything like me. He simply went along with Pappy's instructions. Although I did notice a few changes in him: sometimes he sat in a chair, just staring into space; and when he played the piano the music sounded different, dark and heavy.

Mutti decided to take some of her jewellery to a pawnshop for extra money. I didn't like seeing the shopkeeper take from her hands the treasured gifts that Pappy had given her. The exchange was a ridiculously small sum. It was all so unfair. It reminded me of leaving our home in Vienna. I could hardly believe we had to go through this all over again!

I had planned to tell Heinz all about it, but that afternoon he returned from school very shaken. His friend Walter had taken off his jacket on the way home. The weather was warm and Walter wasn't thinking about the fact that he didn't have a yellow star on his shirt. With his jacket flung over his arm, the yellow star was no longer visible. Two Nazi soldiers stopped Heinz and Walter, and Walter was arrested and taken away. Heinz had also learned earlier in the day that Herman, the boy who had brought me flowers, had been deported with his family. Heinz was in a terrible state. I couldn't help crying myself when I looked at him. Mutti and Pappy tried to reassure him that soon we'd all be safe in hiding.

The preparations were moving along smoothly, but a problem arose that no one had anticipated. I had been off school, not feeling well, and came down with severe tonsillitis. Mutti and Pappy were very worried about me. I needed to have my tonsils taken out, but admission to a hospital was out of the question since the Nazis had begun arresting patients. It wouldn't be easy to get medical help once we went into hiding. So Pappy found a doctor who was willing to operate in his surgery.

I worried about what the doctor would do without the proper medicine, equipment and nurses that they have in hospitals. I was even more scared when it was time for the operation and the doctor tied me down so I couldn't move my arms or legs. The anaesthetic, referred to as laughing gas, put me quickly to sleep but caused me to have weird dreams. I dreamed of a fire with enormous flames that consumed everything around me. Even the air burned and I couldn't escape because I was tied down. I regained consciousness in a terrible state of panic, and everyone had great difficulty calming me down.

When I was finally taken home Mutti, Pappy and Heinz showered me with treats and affection. I refused to eat anything but ice cream, and thought perhaps the ordeal wasn't so bad after all. But eventually Heinz considered the special treatment excessive and told me it was about time I got better. I did enjoy eating normally once again, and having the energy to run and play. Unfortunately, an acute awareness of our grave situation also returned.

On the morning of 6 July 1942 a call-up notice was delivered for Heinz to join thousands of other young people being deported to work camps. Mutti was desperate. Heinz tried to comfort her, though he was surely just as frantic.

'I'll go, Mutti,' he said bravely. 'After all, my friends will be there. Henk, Marcel and Margot probably received cards too, so we will all be together.'

'It will be slave labour,' sobbed Mutti.

'They won't harm me if I work hard,' Heinz said, looking to Pappy for agreement.

'Young people will be useful to them,' Pappy said, 'but I think the time has come for us to disappear.'

Those who took Jews into their homes had to have courage because it put them and their families in terrible danger. Luckily for us, many Dutch people came forward to help. Mutti and I received the address of a teacher, Mrs Klompe, who lived on the other side of Amsterdam. Pappy and Heinz were to stay with a woman called Mrs DeBruin in the country at Soesdijk.

We spent the last few hours together as a family at the kitchen table. Mutti made tea and Pappy retold happy stories of the past, remembering our childhood, and Mutti's and his. Heinz gave me a few words of brotherly advice. I was unusually quiet. We wept and hugged. It was impossible to know what to say as the future was so uncertain.

Then Mutti and I walked out of the front door of our home, on to the street and away from our family's haven. The early-morning light dawned on one of the saddest days I would ever see. My eyes burned with tears of bitterness. We crossed the square where my friends and I had run about and played. I wondered how soon they would miss me. We passed our milkman, who always had a kind word to say, but on this occasion remained silent.

Mutti and I each carried a small bag that held only a few possessions, the ones that Mutti said were most important. We had to leave so many things behind. We had to leave Pappy and Heinz.

I wanted to scream at the soldiers we passed, 'Why are you making us do this? Don't you have a family? Don't you have a heart, or are you just animals?'

When we arrived at our hiding place I felt numb. Mrs Klompe opened the door with a friendly, familiar greeting so that anyone nearby wouldn't become suspicious. 'How are you? It's wonderful to see you again,' she said loudly. 'Come in. Come in.'

Mrs Klompe looked like a proper schoolteacher. Her voice was clear and direct, her words considerate. 'Please, do sit down and have tea,' she said.

Mrs Klompe lived alone. She explained that our rooms were upstairs, and that she would show us around later. She asked Mutti if she would be willing to help with the cooking. I gave Mutti a quick glance to see her reaction, knowing this was not her favourite task. But she agreed willingly, deeply grateful that we had somewhere to stay.

'You cannot use the kitchen or the bathroom while I'm out,' she warned. 'If the neighbours hear any noise they will become suspicious. You will have to take great care to keep your presence here secret.'

'How safe are we?' Mutti wondered aloud.

'The Germans make frequent raids to search out hidden Jews,' Mrs Klompe said. 'They are like rat-catchers intent on exterminating vermin, but we in the Resistance are equally intent on protecting the innocent.'

Mutti spoke solemnly. 'We are greatly indebted to you. Thank you.'

7.

Captured on My Fifteenth Birthday

Mrs Klompe told us about another member of the Dutch Resistance who would stop in to meet us that evening.

'Mr Broeksma is a teaching colleague of mine,' she explained, 'a proud and true Dutchman with fire in his belly. Like all of the underground workers, he is intelligent, reliable and extremely resourceful. You can trust him completely.'

I liked Mr Broeksma immediately. He smiled at us and winked at me. His strong, sturdy voice was comforting.

'You will need another place to hide,' he said, 'in case the apartment is searched.'

Mrs Klompe took us upstairs to inspect our quarters: two small rooms with a place to sleep in each, and a long, narrow bathroom at the end of the hallway. Mr Broeksma examined the rooms carefully, moving a few pieces of furniture and looking down at floorboards and behind doors like he was planning to redecorate.

'We'll put a partition here,' he said to Mutti and Mrs Klompe, pointing to a wall in the small bathroom. 'It will divide the toilet from the rest of the room. Then we'll make a trapdoor about three feet square so there is enough space to climb through. It will be easily concealed in the new tiled wall, and no one will suspect that there is a separate toilet.'

My head was reeling. I could hardly get used to the idea of hiding, staying indoors at all times, not using the bathroom all day long, being perfectly quiet and afraid to move. Then we had to worry about hiding inside the hiding place! But there was nothing I could do. I tried, instead, to realize how fortunate we were for the generosity of our helpers.

The project was completed in a couple of weeks. Mr Broeksma and his friends worked every single night. They had to come after dark, and could only bring a few materials at a time to avoid arousing suspicion. They stayed extra long on the last night, and everyone was relieved to see the job finished.

I was sound asleep when the noise of vans in the street below and heavy knocking at the front door penetrated my dreams and brought me back to reality.

Nazis were downstairs shouting, 'Open up immediately. Let us in.'

'Mutti?' I cried, terrified.

I felt Mutti grab hold of me. 'Quick, Evi, cover the bed with the counterpane,' she whispered.

We hurried to the bathroom and squeezed through the small trapdoor. I crouched down on the floor while Mutti sat on the toilet seat with her legs all folded up. The soldiers stomped through the house, shouting and slamming doors, like the waves of the sea in a great, furious storm, thrashing us against the shore. When they threw open the bathroom door I expected them to hear the pounding of my heart, but they didn't. They also didn't notice the small trapdoor in the tiled wall. As they finally departed, Mrs Klompe shouted her disgust at their invasion of her home.

Mutti and I were stunned, frozen to the spot; we couldn't move for a few minutes. Then we heard Mrs Klompe open the trapdoor and reach in her hand to help us out. I was still shaking. Eventually we went back to bed. Mutti lay down beside me to offer me her comfort, but I could tell she was crying.

Every moment of every day in hiding we worried about being captured. There were brief distractions when I was able to concentrate on a story or lesson or game, but I could never escape the dread, the weight of worry, the sounds lurking in the back of my head of Nazis shouting and crashing into our world.

At night we heard the American and British planes fly overhead on missions to bomb Germany. Everyone expected the war to end quickly after the Americans joined the Allies against Germany. I actually thought I'd be back at school after Christmas, but this did not happen.

Food was rationed, so Mrs Klompe didn't have much to eat. The Resistance found ways to provide for those who had people hiding in their homes. They obtained extra ration cards by raiding offices where they were kept, or printing more themselves. Artists worked meticulously to make authentic-looking copies of these and other official documents.

We appreciated the sacrifices made for us, but were not accustomed to going hungry. I tried to eat slowly and savour what we had, but I just couldn't help thinking about how delicious our kitchen had smelled with a birthday dinner in the oven or a warm chocolate cake on the counter. Sometimes my hunger and frustration got the better of me and I gobbled my food without even tasting it. Mutti didn't say anything; she just gave me a stern look.

Mutti helped me continue my studies in German, French, geography and history. I remembered how much she had enjoyed giving private French lessons in Vienna, yet I had not forgotten her frustration with me in Brussels, so I tried to be diligent and studious. Mrs Klompe generously brought me books and teaching materials. Mr Broeksma came twice a week to help me with Dutch and mathematics. Unfortunately all this attention didn't make studying any easier for me.

I longed to have other students to share the lessons with, to have discussions and debates. I wanted friends who would laugh and joke with me and think of silly things to do. I wanted to run, play and be free. When I dwelled on our circumstances it felt like we were prisoners. Eventually I realized that it was best not to think about it too much.

Monotony hung in the air like a grey cloud that wouldn't lift. There was very little to do but read and study. I had to sit still for hours on end. I had no company except Mutti. I loved my mother, but she could not relate to me the same as someone close to my age. Mutti tried all kinds of tricks to have fun or to focus my attention, but I couldn't overcome the boredom. I ached for Heinz and Pappy.

'What if the Nazis find Heinz and Pappy?' I asked Mutti, anxious to know that they were fine.

Then one day Mutti surprised me with the news that we would soon be spending a weekend with Pappy and Heinz. I was ecstatic! I struggled to contain my excitement and stay quiet and settled. Pappy and Mutti had been planning for weeks, talking briefly on the telephone whenever they could at great risk and great expense. I dreamed of how we would spend our time together. I imagined being outside in the fresh air, with other people, and flowers in bloom.

We began our journey early in the morning. Mutti and I put ourselves in grave danger of being captured, but the visit was very precious and important for our morale, so we took the risk. The fact that we looked like Dutch citizens helped. However, Pappy and Heinz were living in a small town in the country, very near the royal summer palace that the Nazis had turned into one of their headquarters. As we came closer to our destination we had to appear as if we hadn't a care in the world. Actually our stomachs were completely in knots.

Pappy closed the door quickly upon our arrival and Mutti and I cried tears of relief! All of the energy I had been expending to stay safe and hopeful throughout the prior months suddenly melted and I began to sob. Pappy held me until I finally settled down, quietly repeating, 'It's OK, Evi. Everything will be OK.'

Mutti and Pappy exchanged news about the war that they had learned from their hosts: Hitler's armies had surrendered at Stalingrad in Russia and the Allies had gained victories in North Africa.

'Things look a bit more hopeful,' Pappy said encouragingly.

Heinz showed me around, and then we sat in a corner to talk. He knew I would have a lot to say and reminded me that we still had to be quiet. I tried to recall every detail about what I had been doing. My feelings of frustration spilled out, and Heinz let me complain while he listened patiently. I wondered about all of our relatives and friends, but Heinz reminded me that worrying was useless. All we could do was trust that they were fine. Then Heinz tried to cheer me up. He taught me to play chess and we shared our dreams about the day when we would be free again.

At midday Mutti prepared a simple meal, after which our parents taught us to play bridge. Heinz and I struggled at first, but eventually we beat them. We made a good pair! I thought proudly.

Pappy told us how Heinz was determined not to waste any of his time in captivity with idleness, how he had composed serious music, quenched his thirst for knowledge with books in three languages and written poetry. Many of his poems were very sad, but I asked him to recite some of them to us. He spoke each line quietly yet distinctly. I fixed my eyes on his handsome face and listened in awe.

Don't Cry, Mama

Mama, do I have to die already?
I heard the doctor say so.
Please, Mama, don't cry.
Heaven is such a beautiful place
And soon we'll be together again.

Mama, what will my little sister say
When she wants to play with me again?
Please, Mama, don't cry.
After all, I'll be seeing Dad again.
He's been waiting up there so long already.

Remember to take good care of the kitten.
She loves me so.
Please, Mama, don't cry.
Do you still love me as much as ever?
Are you still with me?
Please tell me, Mama.

The worst of it, Mama,
Is that you'll be gone so long.
Please, Mama, don't cry.
There's sure to be a window up there
For me to watch you through.

Please hold my hand for just a minute.
It seems so misty in the room.
Please, Mama, don't cry.
Mama, just one more thing, Mama,
Please kiss me goodbye.

Heinz and Pappy had also been painting. They used any materials they could find: some old brushes, a few containers of paint that they mixed for different colours and a variety of painting surfaces, including dishcloths, tiles and cardboard. Heinz showed us his work proudly. In one painting he had drawn a little child in his playroom. In another he showed an attic room full of old toys, appearing lonely and abandoned, like the apartment we left in Amsterdam.

The most powerful picture told a story of despair. Heinz had painted himself seated at a table with his head resting on his arms as if overcome with sorrow. In the background he portrayed a dying figure. I felt extremely sad looking at this painting, yet totally amazed at Heinz's artistic ability. I had all kinds of questions about Heinz's paintings. 'How do you know what colours to choose? How do you mix the lights and the darks? How do you know what everything looks like when you can't see it?' I asked.

'I just know,' Heinz said, smiling.

Heinz and Pappy made drawings of Mutti and me. Surprisingly, it didn't bother me to sit still for this. In fact, I thought it was rather funny when Heinz kept asking me to turn my head a fraction of an inch this way or that. I wondered what he was thinking when he studied every little detail of my features. *Does Heinz think I look more grown up? Does he think I'm pretty? Does he know how much I look up to him, how much his opinion matters to me, how proud I am of all his talents?* Surprisingly I kept these thoughts to myself.

'I am afraid it is getting late,' Pappy said with a sigh. I clung first to Heinz, then to Pappy, then to Heinz again. Saying goodbye was awful, because we didn't know for sure if any of us would be captured, never to see each other again.

Pappy tried to cheer us up with reminders and encouragement. He instructed me to study hard, listen closely to Mutti and make the most of every minute. He told all of us to hold on to every thread of hope, to make the best of every situation. A picture popped into my head: the links in the chain. I tried to imagine that everything important was connected to some greater good like Pappy promised, not helter-skelter like the upside-down world we were living in.

Mutti's voice became low and solemn when she finally said with a strained firmness, 'Come, Evi, we must go.' We couldn't show any emotion whatsoever as we walked into the street. We had to be extremely careful not to arouse suspicion as we bumped shoulders with our enemy on the train.

Our days turned into weeks and the weeks into months. We managed to visit Pappy and Heinz a few more times. Everyone tried so hard to stay positive as we discussed the bits and pieces of news we had heard: Soviet troops were reclaiming their own country and pushing the Germans back. The British had conducted a massive bombing raid on Hamburg, Germany.

But as the war progressed and the Nazis met with further defeat, they became increasingly determined to carry out their master plan to annihilate all Jews. More and more Jews were deported to the concentration camps, and the Nazis increased the rewards for the capture of those in hiding.

Our hosts became very nervous. Pappy and Heinz felt hostility from Mrs DeBruin, who by then had hidden them for many months. Suddenly, she demanded more money, provided less food, began making rude remarks and insisted that she should have Mutti's fur coat. 'It's quite wasted on you,' she said to Mutti during one of our visits. Mutti had no choice but to hand it over.

Mrs Klompe also became extremely anxious when the Nazis raided her home while we had been away visiting Pappy. She said she was sorry, but she could no longer hide us. She had good reason to be afraid. If we were discovered she would be arrested and sent to one of the concentration camps in Holland. This was not as bad as the death camps in Germany or Poland, but the living conditions were still horrible, and many people died from disease, starvation and hard labour.

The Resistance looked for new hiding places for us, but there were fewer and fewer possibilities. Four years had passed since the Nazi invasion of Holland in 1940! Many Jews had been found and many members of the Resistance had been arrested. They couldn't find us anywhere else to hide so Mutti decided to contact some Christian friends to ask if they knew of a place for us to go. The Reitsmas offered to take us in. Meanwhile, a house had been found for Pappy and Heinz, and we were thrilled to learn that it was very near the Reitsmas. This would make it much easier to arrange visits to see them.

We got together at the first opportunity. Heinz told me all about the journey to their new hiding place. They had left very early in the morning, when there were not too many people out and about. Heinz had dyed his hair blond so he looked more Dutch. A nurse in uniform met them at the station in Amsterdam and led them to their new hosts. The people didn't seem too friendly, but Pappy and Heinz were very glad to be resettled.

Our time together was short, but wonderful. We all felt that our circumstances had greatly improved, and parted on a hopeful note, convinced that the war couldn't last too much longer.

On the morning of my fifteenth birthday, 11 May 1944, Mutti and I were seated for a breakfast celebration. The Reitsmas, our new hosts, had decorated a cheerful table with a vase of tulips and hyacinths. Their twenty-year-old son, Floris, had given me a decorated package as I sat down.

'Keep this as a surprise,' he said. 'You can open it after breakfast.'

Caught up in excitement and anticipation, I almost didn't hear the doorbell. Mrs Reitsma had a puzzled look on her face as she got up to answer it. Nazi soldiers stormed in, shouting and stomping their boots as they entered the room where we sat absolutely stunned.

They pointed guns at us and ordered us to get out. They didn't search for anyone else, but acted like they knew we were there. Mutti pleaded, but they paid no attention. They pushed us out of the house, and forced us to march to the Gestapo headquarters in a former school building a few streets away.

I felt terrified and completely disheartened. Mutti and I had been so sure that we would be safe with our friends. We were led to a room where other captives were sitting in silence. I looked at Mutti and she shook her head in disbelief. It had all happened so quickly. I couldn't work out how the Nazis knew where we were hiding.

The air was heavy with desperation while we sat for hours in a daze. People were taken one by one into a room from which we heard shouting, weeping, screaming and the sounds of beating. I buried my head on Mutti's lap. Suddenly a soldier pointed to Mutti. After she entered the same room, I heard nothing – not a sound.

Then they came for me. As I walked through the doorway I spotted a picture of Hitler on the wall above a table where three Nazis were seated.

'What is your real name? We know you are a Jew,' they shouted, furiously tearing up my false identity papers. 'We want to know about all the people who helped you in hiding. Tell us everything we want to know and you will see your mother, your father and brother as well,' they stated.

Pappy and Heinz have been captured, too? I thought, the words exploding in my consciousness.

My heart felt like it was going to stop with this devastating news. I trembled as they fired questions at me, refusing to answer. Luckily I didn't really know anything about the Reitsmas or any Jewish friends in hiding, for in my fear I might have betrayed them. Eventually they gave up and sent me back to wait.

Then I was interrogated again. They told me that Heinz would be killed if I didn't cooperate. They hit me across my shoulders and back with a large club. I tried not to scream, but eventually a sound came out of me that I had never heard before.

At long last I was taken to another room where I found not only Mutti and the Reitsmas, but Heinz and Pappy. We collapsed into each other's arms, devastated by the events that had unfolded.

'Why?' I sobbed. 'We didn't do anything wrong. How did they find out about us?'

'I'm afraid the nurse who met us at the train station was working for the Nazis. She had someone follow you to the Reitsmas' house after your visit. Our new hosts were double agents too. They must have planned all along to betray us. So much suffering and agony in exchange for a reward of five guilders per person – it is incomprehensible!'

Pappy looked crestfallen. He felt that he had let us down and he could no longer do anything to protect us.

Mutti felt extremely sorry for the Reitsmas who had

been arrested for helping us. They were elderly and would never survive in a concentration camp. Pappy told the Nazi officers he would tell them where we had hidden our jewellery if they let the Reitsmas go free, and to our great amazement they kept to their word.

'Why can't they let us go free, too?' Heinz asked.

Pappy looked at him with resignation. 'I suppose it is because they think we are the enemy,' he said sadly.

Although the sun had risen on my birthday, it was the darkest day of my life.

8.

Cast into Darkness

Mutti, Pappy, Heinz and I were ordered out of the building. The Nazi soldier pointed his gun at us and shouted for us to sit in the back of a black van that was already crowded with victims of all ages, bruised and weeping. We were taken to the local Dutch prison. I felt numb, exhausted and helpless, like a piece of driftwood being tossed about in a rough sea. My shoulder was sore from the beating, but I tried not to cry about it. Mutti had her arm around me the entire way and Heinz's head was on Pappy's shoulder. When we arrived, prison guards sent the men in one direction and the women in another.

Mutti couldn't take her eyes off Pappy, who continued to look her way until the last moment possible.

Before he disappeared he mouthed a message, 'Chin up,' and gave a thumbs-up signal to assure us that everything would work out.

We were taken to a dormitory crowded with mothers, crying babies, grandmothers and young girls like me. Most kept to themselves. I clung to Mutti, afraid of what might happen next.

'What are we doing in prison?' I said to Mutti. She held me tighter but didn't respond.

A woman named Franzi moved from bunk to bunk, sharing kind words of comfort. She came to Mutti and me and explained that we should all look after each other and help one another when possible. Franzi's kindness made me think of a time that Heinz was bullied at school and one of his classmates helped him feel better by saying they could stick together. I felt a little reassurance, but couldn't ignore the memories of my birthday nor the sight of desperation all around us.

I realized that my family belonged to a helpless group of people, picked on, discriminated against, bullied, tortured, for one reason only – because we were Jewish. Many, including Mutti and Pappy, trusted that goodness and righteousness still existed enough to prevent a catastrophe. They believed that things would ultimately get better, that people would realize how evil Hitler was and stop supporting him. It was terrifying to think of how bad things had become, and how big Hitler's power had grown, how it seemed to have changed the whole world. I just stayed close to Mutti and held on to the assurance that Pappy and Heinz were nearby.

The following morning a guard read from a list the names of prisoners going to Westerbork, a Dutch transit camp where Jews were held before being sent on to Germany or Poland. It included Mutti and me. He told us to gather our few possessions, and then commanded us to march down the road to the train station. Luckily we found Heinz and Pappy there. At least we were still together. We clasped hands to avoid being separated, while the Nazi guards ordered us on to the train. They stood at every exit and door with guns in hand, leaving no chance for escape.

We sat crowded together in an ordinary compartment of an ordinary train, but our journey was anything but ordinary. We were hungry, bewildered, and terribly afraid. The guards stood over us, clad in black uniforms with tall, black, shiny boots. They watched our every move and shouted orders. The train sped past farmers tilling their fields and women planting spring gardens. I longed to be outside. I could smell and taste freedom just outside the window. I yearned for trips to the mountains and family gatherings in Vienna so long, long ago.

We arrived at Westerbork when the afternoon sun was beginning to set. The conditions of the camp appeared primitive; the prisoners watching us arrive looked worried and anxious, but not hopeless. The administrators and supervisors were Jews. While their orders came from the Nazis, they showed us compassion and allowed us to keep a small suitcase of clothing from the Reitsmas. Most importantly, we were permitted to spend our days with Pappy and Heinz.

Heinz tried to help me pass the time by retelling some of the stories we loved. We found a bit of shade where we could sit and rest. I leaned against my big brother, closed my eyes and let his soothing voice carry me back to the comfort of our earlier years.

Mutti stayed busy, helping wherever it was needed. Pappy continued to think of our safety. He found friends who worked in the camp, and spoke to them about finding essential jobs for us so we wouldn't be deported to the concentration camps in the East. We knew that terrible things were happening there, that Jews were actually being gassed and killed.

A few days later we heard about a train leaving Westerbork that would take people to Poland, most likely to one of the death camps. We tried to keep our spirits up, and reassured ourselves that the Nazis wouldn't send us on the train if we worked hard. Pappy gave us lectures on survival. He told us to try to get as much rest as possible to keep our strength up and be sure to help each other along.

'And always wash your hands to avoid the possibility of germs or sickness,' he especially emphasized. This made Heinz and me smile a little, despite our dire situation.

Later I asked Heinz, 'Does Pappy really think we'll be separated? That's what it sounds like. He was giving directions like he wasn't going to be with us. Heinz, I just couldn't bear it!'

His eyes were full of tears as he answered me. 'I think this is possible. It's happened to so many other families. But I really don't know for sure.'

That night I dreamed that I had been abandoned in a dark place. Everything around me was unfamiliar. The people had unidentifiable features and a blank expression that revealed no purpose or direction. I wanted to run, but I didn't know which way to go.

I woke with a start, my hands clammy and my breathing shaky. I was relieved when I realized that it had all been a dream. Mutti lay beside me, and I calmed down to the rhythm of her even breathing. I stared into the night for a long time, wondering when the daylight would return.

Pappy, Mutti, Heinz and I had prayed for us to remain at Westerbork, but the deportation list included our names. On a hot day in mid May we were forced on to the cattle cars of a train, like animals being sent to slaughter. More than a hundred people were crowded in so tightly that no one had room to sit, much less lie down. The four of us hung on to one another, desperately afraid of being separated. We travelled for three days with hardly any food or water. People groaned, whimpered, wept; hardly anyone spoke. I felt as if we had become participants in a tragic drama for which there was no exit.

At one point Heinz whispered to me, 'I want to tell you about our paintings, Evi. You remember, the ones Pappy and I made when we were in hiding?'

Heinz explained that he and Pappy had hidden them under the floorboards in Mrs DeBruin's house.

'I tucked a note inside, explaining that we will come back after the war to retrieve them,' he said.

His thoughts seemed far away, yet I could detect a tiny bit of excitement in his voice as he described the pictures to me.

'I really want you to see them,' he said. 'I think you'll like what I have done.'

Despite our hopeless circumstances I smiled, and in that moment felt nothing but the utmost pride and affection for Heinz. I knew that he was terrified about what was going to happen to us, but he tried not to show it. He wanted to be the big brother and protect me from my fears.

When the train came to a stop, Mutti got out first and handed me her coat and felt hat, insisting that I must put it on since I might not be allowed to keep my suitcase. It was warm and I didn't want to wear it, but Pappy said I looked like a smart young lady so I cooperated.

Within moments everyone realized that we had arrived at Auschwitz-Birkenau, a death camp in Poland. There was shouting, screaming and chaos, with thousands of people teeming on a small platform. Some families had been in separate train cars and people were running around, trying to find each other. Everyone was nervous, anxious and sick from the journey.

Nazi guards with batons and vicious dogs were shouting, 'Leave all your belongings on the platform. Women to this side, men over there. Stand in rows of five.'

Heinz and I hugged one another as if we would never let go. Mutti and Pappy held each other desperately. Then Mutti embraced Heinz, her beautiful artistic son, while Pappy grasped my hand and looked deeply into my eyes.

'God will protect you, Evi,' he said with all the love in the world. Then he and Heinz were forced to walk away.

9.

Lost in a Nightmare

The immense complex of Auschwitz–Birkenau, built around the small Polish town of Oświęcim, encompassed nearly twenty-five square miles. The area designated for the men was called Auschwitz; the area for the women, Birkenau. Row upon row of long barracks covered the barren land. Miles of electrified barbed wire outlined the perimeter.

Nazis with guns paraded among us, while others stood back sneering. One particular officer stood out. He wore white gloves and had a small baton in his hand. His name was Dr Mengele. We later learned that he was known as 'the angel of death'. In a single glance he decided if a person would live or die, judging simply by how they looked or how he felt.

'You go to the right, you to the left,' he indicated with his little baton.

That's all it took for someone to be condemned to death. All the older people and children and most of the girls my age were told to stand on the left. Eventually this entire group was marched unsuspectingly to gas chambers that they thought were shower rooms. They were handed bars of soap, a final brutal trick to mislead them. Within a few minutes everyone was dead. Miraculously, I was spared. I wondered if it had anything to do with the coat and hat that Pappy had said made me look 'like a smart young lady'.

One mother stepped out of line to follow her child. A guard grabbed her arm and threw her to the ground, then hit her with his baton. I shuddered with shock and disbelief. I held on tight to Mutti's hand, and imagined that Heinz was holding on to Pappy. I tried to blank out everything that was happening, and fill my mind with Pappy's reassurances:

Nothing gets lost . . . Everything is connected . . . The chain cannot be broken . . . In that moment, surrounded by desperation and suffering at the entrance to a death camp, Pappy's promise gave me hope.

We quickly lost our individuality. Mutti and I found ourselves amongst a group of Dutch women, all in a middle-age range except for me; I was the youngest. A special group of prisoners, most of them Polish, were put in charge of us. They were called Kapos. They often acted with cruelty, expecting people to move unreasonably fast and then hitting them if they didn't. They got their orders from the Nazis, who walked around making inspections to see that everything was done properly. The Nazis also made the 'selections', determining who would live and who would die.

The Kapos ordered us to undress. Mortified and embarrassed, I dared not think about how I felt or I wouldn't have been able to move. My actions became mechanical. Mutti offered encouraging glances, but tears streamed down her cheeks. My beautiful hair was all cut off, and so was hers. I almost didn't recognize her.

We were shoved into a shower room, terrified that the pipes would release poisonous gas. Instead the water trickled over our trembling bodies, washing away the happiness of our past lives. As we exited we were each thrown a thin, drab garment and two unmatched shoes that didn't fit our feet. These would be our only possessions. We never even had a piece of toilet paper.

Then everyone had to have their arm tattooed with a long number. When it was my turn Mutti pleaded with the Kapo to make the numbers small. Surprisingly she did. It was the only act of kindness I ever encountered in the camp. After this we marched to the barracks like a flock of lost sheep just shorn. Each one looked no different from the next. The Kapos in charge told us where we would sleep, crowded in rows of bunks like sardines. By that time we were too hungry and distraught to care.

It didn't take long before we lost all sense of time, had no awareness of the month or day of the week. Holidays and birthdays simply didn't exist. Every waking moment felt the same: dark, dreadfully frightening and completely exhausting. We got up for roll-call long before sunrise and went to bed long after dark.

It was early summer 1944 and we had no awareness of what was happening with the war. For the prisoners struggling to survive in a concentration camp, the world seemed to be growing smaller and smaller, like the flame of a candle about to go out.

In fact, US, British and Canadian troops had launched a major offensive on the coast of France, defeating the Germans in Western Europe. The Soviets were defeating them in the East. But in the death camp it wouldn't have made much difference if we had known.

Like every prisoner, I was required to do harsh work or face death. For a time I had to carry big boulders of rock from one place to another. Mutti walked behind me in tears, heartbroken to see her little girl suffer such brutality while she could do nothing to help.

For three weeks Mutti and I were assigned a different job, which was not so hard physically, but emotionally it was excruciating. It was located in the sorting camp, nicknamed 'Canada' because it stood for 'plenty' and 'freedom'. The work entailed the sad task of sorting the belongings of all the prisoners, the new arrivals and some who were already dead. Thousands of people, mostly Jews, were brought to Auschwitz–Birkenau every single day. All their possessions were taken away, just like ours had been. We had to search through enormous piles of clothing, opening the hems of all the garments, looking for hidden valuables. People had hoped to bribe their way out of the camp with their treasures, jewellery, wedding rings, money and even medals from the First World War. Instead, we sorted all the items into enormous heaps for shipment to Germany. We found precious photos of sweet children, adorable babies and proud grandparents whom everyone knew had been killed. If it had not been for the Kapos, shouting at us to get on with our work, we would have all sat there crying.

We had no chance to make friends in the camp, no time for relaxation or the opportunity to recover a little energy. We had nothing. We lived in the moment, believing it was only a matter of time until we might starve, contract dysentery, typhus or cholera, or be selected to perish in the gas chambers like so many others.

The Nazis made our situation unbearable. We were plagued by lice and bedbugs, which led to uncontrollable scratching and inevitable infection. Disease was rampant. We longed for nourishing food and clean water; each day brought only a small ration of bread and a little watery soup, only about three hundred calories. The hunger was so intense that my whole body hurt, not just my stomach. I could feel it, even in my sleep. When we woke in the morning we often found people dead in our bunks, and many collapsed throughout the day. The Nazis figured that a person could last no more than twelve weeks. Hundreds of thousands died, and those who survived grew increasingly weak. They weren't worried about the loss of labour because they would be transporting more Jews to replace them.

We noticed that the Nazis kept at a safe distance from us. They didn't make eye contact with anyone. They treated us like animals and called us things like vermin or swine. They also used clever words to describe their actions in order to hide the truth. The Jews from Poland were told they were being 'resettled', when in fact they were brought to concentration camps to be killed. They referred to their plan to murder all the Jews as the 'final solution'.

Some of the Nazis on duty lived with their families just outside the camp. After sending hundreds of Jewish parents and children to their death in the gas chambers, they went home to read stories to their own children, or sit down to a family meal. They even went to church!

'I don't understand how people can act this way. They call us animals, Mutti, but they are the ones who are animals, not us!' I said one night. 'Why doesn't God do something? So many people are suffering. When will God hear our prayers? Maybe God doesn't even exist.'

'I wish I had answers for you, Evi,' Mutti said sadly, 'but some things cannot be explained. We must do the best we can each day. Remember what Pappy told us about taking care of each other?'

I nodded, and then fell into an exhausted sleep.

Somehow I never lost hope or the will to live. If a person thought for one second that there was no hope of survival, they quickly declined. Their bodies simply couldn't continue to fight.

Mutti's presence throughout this time was like a ray of light. Her look, her touch, her words connected me to the past, to home, to family, to my identity. She often insisted that I take her bread ration, and very quickly became even thinner than the rest of us. Yet, somehow she remained strong and kept up her spirits so she would be able to help me. When we collapsed in our bunks to go to sleep she soothed my sore muscles and comforted me. Mutti gave me courage and strength, and in turn my presence gave her a purpose to live.

'I'm worried,' I told Mutti with a heavy feeling in my chest. 'How do you think Heinz is doing? I don't know how he can manage if he is as hungry as me. A boy needs more food. He must keep up his strength.'

'Pappy will try to look after him as best he can,' Mutti reassured me.

'I wonder what work Heinz and Pappy have to do,' I rambled on. 'Do you think Heinz was chosen to play the piano in the orchestra? I hope not. That would be so terrible, having to entertain the Nazis. I miss Heinz, Mutti. I miss him so much!'

'We must hope that Heinz and Pappy have each other, like you and I do.'

We had no opportunity to take care of our health and hygiene. A huge boil developed on my neck that became extremely painful. It kept getting worse and I contracted severe diarrhoea and a very high fever. I didn't want to go to the hospital barracks because most people didn't return. Even though there were doctors there in white coats, it was all a trick because no one wanted us to get better. There was no place for people to be healed. The hospital barracks just isolated those who were sick until they died or were sent to the gas chambers. Nevertheless, Mutti decided that my condition had become too serious, that I might have the symptoms of typhus, and we had to seek help. After much debate I finally agreed.

To our great joy and astonishment, Mutti recognized her cousin, Minni, working at the hospital as a nurse. She had been sent to Auschwitz-Birkenau from another camp in Czechoslovakia. Her husband, a reputable skin specialist, treated the Nazis, so Minni was in a safe position and could occasionally make special arrangements for others. Minni made certain that I was not admitted to the hospital, but instead got some medication for me. I had contracted typhus, and without her care I surely would have died.

Mutti's discovery of Minni among hundreds of thousands of people was really a miracle. We thought this must have some special meaning for us. It served as an important sign of hope.

Then one terrible day Mutti was taken from me. She had been selected with a group of other prisoners to be murdered in the gas chambers. I stood and watched her being led away, tears of hopelessness streaming down my face, powerless to do anything about it. From that moment on I started to doubt that I would be able to carry on much longer. I trudged through day after day in a fog of despair, completely alone, numb, unable to think and afraid to dream. I thought that my final end would soon come, too.

Yet, amazingly, in the midst of my loneliness and desperation I remembered Pappy's powerful promise and realized his love was not far away.

Everything is connected, like a chain that cannot be broken, he had said.

When we were in the mountains he always told me

not to focus on how steep the climb, but look forward to where we were going. Somehow the memory of Pappy's vitality and encouragement penetrated the hard, cold shell of desolation and I managed to pull through that terrible time.

I dared not think about all that I had lost in the six months since I had turned fifteen. Some days, while moving through the camp with a work unit, I passed groups of people on their way to the gas chambers. I looked at their faces and knew they would soon be dead, but I couldn't feel anything. We barely had enough energy for ourselves.

One bitter afternoon I sat in a work unit assigned to make rope. We tore pieces of material into large strips with our teeth, and then braided them into plaits. My feet kept a steady rhythm stamping the frozen ground to stay warm. Suddenly the Kapo walked up behind me and instructed me to go outside. She said that someone wanted to see me. I hesitated to get up, afraid to be hurt or taken away, but knew I had no choice in the matter. I stepped outside the building and with great trepidation looked up to see that there was a person waiting for me.

'Pappy!' I cried in disbelief.

My father stood before me in a striped blue and grey prison suit and cap. His wasted body and baldness shocked me, but I was so ecstatic to see him. When he held me the weight of the whole world vanished.

'Evi, don't cry,' he said, lifting my face up and wiping away my tears. 'Everything will work out.'

We were silent for a few minutes. Then he asked me about Mutti and I could hardly speak. I whispered only a few words before he realized what I was struggling to say, that I thought Mutti had been killed.

'No,' he cried, in a long, slow, painful moan. His strength seemed to leave him and he clutched his chest.

A feeling of panic struck me that Pappy could die too, that I could be left totally alone.

But then he turned to meet my gaze and said quietly yet resolutely, 'We must be brave, Evi. We will soon be free and together again, you and me and Heinz.'

'Heinz . . . oh, Pappy, is he OK?' I said.

I had not mentioned Heinz at all, afraid to ask in case something terrible had happened to him.

'He's quite well,' Pappy said. 'He's working in a garden growing all kinds of vegetables. The fresh air and exercise are doing him good, and you should see how tall he has grown. But, of course, he has also become very thin.'

Pappy's eyes came back to life as he explained further.

'I have a proper job. I am in charge of the office in a wood factory near here, and you can see I've gained permission to come and find you. I'll come again, Evi, I promise.' Then he said, with the old mischievous twinkle in his eye, 'Now I will go to the kitchen and arrange for somebody there to let you have a little extra food whenever possible.'

Pappy kissed me farewell, and promised to see me again. My faith in him was absolute. I returned to my work, amazed that Pappy had managed to find me, astonished that he could arrange for a favour – extra food! I was convinced that at last everything might start to improve.

The Kapos treated me somewhat better from that day on. I received a little extra food from a girl in the kitchen, and the hollow feeling of hunger that gnawed at my insides day and night subsided a little.

Pappy came to see me one more time. He told me that Heinz was coping and that he was sure the war couldn't last much longer. Soon our suffering would come to an end. As we parted, Pappy and I exchanged looks of such yearning and love that I have seen his face like this in my dreams throughout my life.

Pappy had strengthened my will to survive, and I considered myself extremely lucky not to be one of the countless people who had given up the will to go on. Week after week the icy cold winter wind tore through the thin walls of the unheated barracks and penetrated our light clothing. Our bodies railed against the relentless dampness and chill. Huge piles of snow were never cleared. No matter how severe the weather became, all the prisoners still had to stand outside for hours to be counted at the beginning and end of each day – thousands of prisoners counted many times over, first by the Kapos, then by the Nazis. Why did they bother? The number kept changing because people were constantly dying. Sickness descended on the camp like a black cloud. My toes and fingers suffered terrible frostbite. Yet, miraculously, I held on.

One evening, as I was slowly eating my small piece of

bread, a group of Dutch women suddenly stopped in front of me. They all began talking at the same time.

'Eva? Oh, Eva, thank God we found you, and you are still alive! We have just come from the hospital barracks. Your *mutti* is there. She is still alive!'

Mutti's cousin, Minni, was still working as a nurse for the head doctor, Dr Mengele. She must have intervened so that Mutti would be spared from the gas chambers. For three long months I had thought she was dead.

I wanted to shout with joy. I wanted to run to Mutti and tell her that I had seen Pappy, that he and Heinz were both alive. I wanted to find Pappy and tell him the wonderful news. But we were still captives, and it would be impossible for me to go to the hospital to see Mutti. I could do nothing but wait and hope.

'Soon we will be together again,' I said to myself repeatedly throughout the days that followed, and the thought lulled me to sleep each night.

As the end of 1944 approached we began to notice some changes. We heard bombing in the distance and sensed that the Nazis were nervous. They weren't running the camp with the same efficiency, and the overall discipline had become more lax. They realized that the Russian troops were approaching, so they blew up the crematoria and the gas chambers, hoping to hide their terrible crimes of the previous years.

In the meantime, the winter had taken its toll on my toes. The frostbite became so bad that I could hardly walk.

I had no choice but to apply for permission to go to the hospital barracks. Mutti was still there and I hoped that by some chance I would be able to see her. Fortunately, I found Minni, who took care of my admission and, to my great elation, arranged for me to stay in the same bunk with Mutti.

I found Mutti extremely weak and emaciated. At first she couldn't believe her eyes when she saw me standing before her, my cheeks red from the cold outside as well as from my great excitement. But when I lay down on the bunk beside her, the tears of happiness turned to sorrow.

She felt my bones and my emaciated body and cried, 'Oh, my dear Evi, you are so thin.'

I assured her that I was coping, that we would both be all right since we were together again. I told her that I had been receiving a little extra food because of Pappy.

'Erich!' Mutti sighed.

Then I went on to tell her all about my incredible visits from Pappy and his reports about how Heinz had been tending a garden. I shared every detail about how Pappy looked, every word he spoke, how he held me and how I had felt to be with him. I could hardly talk fast enough, and Mutti could hardly contain her excitement. We talked endlessly in whispers about all that had happened in the three months we had been apart, and marvelled at the miracle of how Mutti's life had been saved through Minni's intervention.

Many times during that period Mutti drifted into a

kind of daze, sighing over and over, 'Oh, Erich. Oh, my sweet Heinz.' Her eyes were closed as if she were lost in a dream of happy times.

Gradually my condition improved, and I began to realize that our roles had reversed. Mutti didn't have any strength left to look after me; instead I had to look after her. Mutti was struggling to stay alive, and she needed me. I considered this a very important time in my life, for Mutti and I recognized that I had grown up.

One morning in January 1945 we awoke to a deadening silence. All the Nazis, guard dogs and Kapos had left in the night, taking most of the prisoners with them, including Minni. The Russian army was advancing across Poland, so the Nazis were taking tens of thousands of prisoners into the camps in Germany and Austria. Thousands of weakened captives marched for miles in the dead of winter with only bits of bread, thin clothing, some without shoes. Many collapsed and were shot. Many froze. Few survived.

Mutti and I had been left in the hospital to die with about three hundred others in such a critical condition that the Nazis considered them already dead. Some perished within days, but little by little we grew stronger. Still, we were in a state of desolation and confusion. We could hear the sounds of fierce fighting nearby, but we couldn't understand what was happening. We hoped that the Russians were approaching but we had no way of knowing. We didn't realize then that Italy, France and Belgium had been freed, that the Nazis were being attacked from all sides and that the war in Europe was nearing the end. We could only think about staying warm and finding food and water.

10.

Found with the End in Sight

I joined a small group of weak but capable prisoners who
ventured out of the hospital wrapped in blankets. We were
terribly afraid that the Nazis might suddenly reappear.
But our need for food and water spurred us on. We made
our way to the kitchen block, and to our great amazement
and delight found mounds of black bread. We carried as
much as possible, passed it out to everyone, even those
too sick to eat. Then I found Mutti and collapsed on our
bunk from the little bit of energy I had exerted. Eventually
we found more food, cheese, potatoes and clothing! We
put on boots that fitted our feet, and coats that hung like
sacks. Obtaining drinking water was a problem, but in
our desperation we found tools and energy to break
through the ice on the pond just outside the gates.

One day a Russian scout appeared who looked at first
like a great big bear. He was followed by groups of soldiers,
just passing through on their way to the Front where they
would continue the important task of forcing the Germans
out of Poland. For the most part they left us alone. We
couldn't understand each other because we spoke different
languages, and they couldn't afford the time to stop and

help. However, they did share their soup with us – nourishing, hot and absolutely delicious.

Over the next few days more groups of Russians came and went, during which time we expended all our energy on the first steps of recovery. The only tasks we could manage were obtaining food and water, eating, staying warm and resting. We felt no sense of comfort or relief. And although the Nazis had left the camp we were not yet safe.

Somehow I imagined that Pappy would be able to send someone to rescue us, but he had no way of knowing that Mutti and I had been left behind. We would have to find help ourselves. The thought was terrifying. It was the dead of winter and we were in a foreign land in the midst of a war zone. Nonetheless, we covered ourselves in a mound of warm clothing and, wrapped up in blankets, moved in a huddled mass outside the front gate of Birkenau. We followed a road that was barely visible as snow had drifted over the path. The icy wind made it nearly impossible to stay upright while we moved ever so slowly in what we desperately hoped was the right direction. Finally, after hours that felt like days, we arrived at the men's camp of Auschwitz. The Russians had set up a temporary headquarters there. Right away I asked everyone if they had seen Pappy and Heinz, or if they had heard their names, 'Erich and Heinz Geiringer', but they sadly shook their heads. Unfortunately, we couldn't help them either with information about their loved ones.

One man looked slightly familiar.

'Do we know each other?' I asked. 'My name is Eva Geiringer.'

'I am Otto Frank,' he responded.

'Oh yes, of course. You are Anne and Margot's father.'

He looked very old, and his face was tight and weary. However, I could see kindness in his eyes. He asked me if I knew anything about Mrs Frank or his daughters, Anne and Margot, but I didn't.

Eventually the Russians decided it was not safe for any of the survivors to stay in Auschwitz. The war was still going on, and the Germans could come back. So the Russians took us on trains eastwards away from the enemy. We witnessed terrible ruin everywhere, villages and towns where people emerged from piles of rubble. Nothing remained. Everything had been destroyed.

Although we travelled further and further away from the Nazis, our extreme weakness made it impossible for us to comprehend and be happy about our survival. We had been hungry for so long that it was difficult to eat properly. Some people ate too much or too quickly and became violently ill. Some even died. I was not always careful and I did get quite sick on one occasion, but Mutti made sure that it didn't happen again.

The Russians had very little provisions, but whatever they had, they shared with us. We still slept on the floor and travelled in cattle trucks, but the Russians did whatever they could to make us comfortable. Most importantly, we knew from their kindness that someone cared.

On 7 May 1945 Germany surrendered. The war in Europe was over! Four days later Mutti declared a celebration. It was my sixteenth birthday. By that time we were staying on an estate in Odessa on the Black Sea with concentration camp survivors, forced labourers from Holland, France and Italy and liberated prisoners of war from as far away as Australia. The place had once been the summer home of a Russian prince, and although emptied of furniture and completely bare, it was still absolutely exquisite.

Of course, I didn't have a real party with cake, music and dancing but I did receive special gifts. Kea, a Dutch girl also aged sixteen, had made a necklace for me of shells. Bill, a tall and handsome Australian soldier who flirted with Mutti, gave me a bar of chocolate. Peace was the best gift of all. Still, I had one more wish that I prayed with all my heart would be granted: that Pappy and Heinz were safe and well and also on their way home.

On 15 May a troop transport ship from New Zealand docked in the port of Odessa and welcomed us aboard. At long last we were headed for Holland!

I entered our cabin first.

'Look, Mutti, our room is absolutely perfect!'

I hugged a feather pillow and ran my hand along the crisp white sheet and the velvety soft blanket.

'Yes, this is incredible!' Mutti responded.

When we walked into the dining room, Mutti burst into tears.

'China dishes and silver, just for us!' she said. 'I can't believe it!'

All the tables were set with white linen napkins, silver-plated cutlery, china dishes and crystal glasses. We were being treated like human beings again, and could finally accept that we were free.

We sailed across the Black Sea into the Mediterranean, west of Turkey, south of Greece and Italy, to the coast of France. As we disembarked, the local people welcomed us with flowers, music, food and wine. We continued our journey home by train through France and Belgium. These countries had suffered extensive ruin, yet people greeted us with a warm reception at each station.

Once we crossed the border into Holland we were taken to a convent, and were terribly disappointed to learn that we couldn't continue straight on to Amsterdam. The bridges over the big rivers had all been destroyed. We had to wait a few days while pontoon bridges were built and further transportation could be arranged.

As groups of survivors arrived from different places, I looked for Pappy and Heinz.

I asked everyone, 'Have you heard the names Heinz and Erich? I'm looking for my father and brother.'

I wondered how tall Heinz had grown, and if he would look more like a man than a boy. *Would he think I had changed? Would he look at me and know that I was different, that I had grown up, that I had even taken care of Mutti in the hospital and helped her get well? Would Pappy know that I had tried hard to follow all his instructions, and that I had remembered all his words of advice and his promise to Heinz and me?*

We heard traumatic stories of loss, and my heart seemed to stop with each report of a brother or father who had been killed. I marvelled that Mutti and I had been able to survive. We had been through a horrendous experience, yet we had been extremely fortunate.

Throughout the week I had many questions for Mutti.

'How did we manage to stay together?' I asked after hearing countless stories of families completely torn apart.

'I don't know,' she said. 'We were very fortunate.'

'Why did I survive when most children my age were sent directly to the gas chambers?' I asked.

'I don't know, Evi,' Mutti replied.

'How did you ever find Minni in such a big place with all those people? Neither of us would have lived if it weren't for Minni,' I exclaimed.

'I know. It was some kind of miracle,' she answered.

'Then why didn't everyone else get the miracles they needed?' I went on. 'And how did Pappy ever manage to find me, not once, but twice? And how did I escape the death march? I wasn't sick like you, Mutti. I could have been taken with everyone else.'

'I know,' Mutti said. 'It is beyond our understanding.'

Our survival couldn't be explained. A small number of Jews had escaped to free countries or had managed to stay hidden throughout the war, but very few survived the concentration camps.

Finally I realized that we were actually on our way home.

'Home, home,' I said repeatedly like a mantra. 'We are going home.'

I didn't know what to expect. I started to feel a bit afraid that all of our possessions would be gone, that we would have to start from the beginning to rebuild our home. But I also realized that home was not the place where we used to live, or the collection of things we had gathered. Home was our family: Heinz, Pappy, Mutti and me together, at the start and end of every day.

My constant anxiety about Pappy and Heinz grew into a deep ache that wouldn't subside. At night I looked up at the stars and sent my prayers towards the heavens. Like shooting stars, they flew over the confusion and destruction to keep Heinz and Pappy safe and bring them home.

11.

Uplifted by the Gift of Hope

My heart beat faster as we approached the outskirts of Amsterdam. Mutti and I longed to find someone we could talk to, someone that knew us. We needed human contact, not just an empty apartment. So we made our first stop at the home of our close friends, the Rosenbaums. Rosi was a Christian and we hoped that she would be there, and that Martin had managed to escape the Nazis.

Martin's face lit up when he opened the front door and found us standing before him. We embraced with great exhilaration, but Martin gasped when he realized that we must have been in one of the concentration camps since we were so thin.

'Erich . . . Heinz?' he said, his eyes full of concern.

Mutti shook her head.

'We are hoping . . .' was all she could say.

We asked about Rosi. To our great surprise and delight Martin told us that she was in the hospital with a new baby, a son!

The miracle of new life seeped into my pores like a healing balm. When Rosi came home with the tiny baby, I ran my fingers across his silky skin, so soft and warm.

I watched his face wrinkle and his eyes narrow as he fixed his attention on my face, looking like he had found something of serious interest. Martin talked constantly to him, so thrilled and proud to have a son. I loved to look at Rosi and Mutti as they took turns rocking him to sleep. He curled peacefully in their arms, as if there was no other place in the world.

When we returned to our apartment on the Merwedeplein we were astonished to find all of our possessions still there. Everything appeared the same: the furniture, the curtains; the decor had not changed one bit. How odd it felt to walk from room to room, sensing all that was familiar, while acutely aware of the endless months we had spent lost in a totally different and horrible world. I cried at the sight of Pappy's pencil markings on the wall where he had recorded our growth. Heinz would surely have grown taller than Mutti in the time that had passed.

I, too, had grown since then, but in ways that I didn't choose. I was more aware of the cruel behaviour adults were capable of. I had seen children mistreat each other in the playground but I had never imagined that grown-ups would do the same, that they would become so full of hatred. It turned the whole world upside down, and brought chaos and devastation into every home.

Mutti and I both struggled to regain our health. I had trouble with my toes because of the frostbite I had contracted in the camp. I couldn't digest heavy foods, but had to stay on a plain diet of pasta, rice and mashed potatoes for a long time. Mutti had digestive problems as well. Our physical pain would have been more bearable if we had only had word from Pappy and Heinz. Day after day we checked the lists of people who had been found, but their names were never included.

One morning as we sat at the breakfast table, Mutti spoke to me about playing with my food. 'You're far too skinny,' she said.

Suddenly we both felt a flood of memories: Pappy telling Mutti not to worry about my weight, Heinz teasing me about having to take castor oil, Heinz appeasing me with stories . . .

'When will Heinz be home?' I cried. 'It's too quiet here. I can't stand it.'

Mutti cried too.

'Will things ever get better? Will we ever be happy again?' I continued, feeling miserable.

Mutti shook her head slowly and said, 'I don't know how we will manage, Evi, but we will face whatever lies ahead together. For now, let us focus on the good that still exists. People need our help, so let us do as Pappy always suggested – let us take care of others.'

We took in two lady lodgers who had nowhere to go. They were extremely grateful and helped us a little with the rent. Gradually Mutti and I returned to a regular routine – me to school and Mutti to a new job. Martin Rosenbaum hired Mutti to be his secretary at the tie factory, which was quite a challenge as she had never learned to type. Every evening she came home with a big parcel. At first I got excited, thinking she had brought home a surprise. Instead it was a stack of papers that she had spoiled with errors. She didn't dare throw them away in the office, as paper was expensive and difficult to come by, and she didn't want to lose her position! Eventually Mutti became quite proficient.

One day a short letter arrived in the mail from the Red Cross. Mutti called me to sit with her at the kitchen table, suspecting the contents contained the news we had been dreading so long to hear. Fear already filled her eyes.

The message was brief: 'After the forced march from Auschwitz, Heinz Geiringer died from exhaustion in April 1945 at Mauthausen. Erich Geiringer died on 4 May 1945, at Mauthausen' – one day before the camp was liberated by the Americans, three days before the end of the war and only one week before my sixteenth birthday.

All our hopes vanished in an instant. Devastation, shock and agony mixed with disbelief, filling every corner of the apartment. Mutti sat at the table for hours holding the letter.

I walked around the apartment in a daze, repeating over and over, 'It can't be true. It just can't be true.'

Heinz and Pappy had suffered all those months at Auschwitz, then were forced to walk for miles in the freezing winter wind, starved and emaciated, from Poland all the way across Czechoslovakia to Austria. They spent their last moments in one of the cruellest concentration camps, only hours from Vienna, completely unaware of our survival.

My mind wouldn't let me believe the truth. Then I uncovered Pappy's hiking boots in the front hall cupboard, and I saw an image of him resting on a large boulder in the mountains, smiling at me while I talked non-stop about our adventures. Grief cut through me like a sharp knife as I registered the fact that his boots were still there, but he was not.

Anger welled up in me like a tornado tearing across an open plain, increasing in magnitude, twisting out of control. It was all so unfair!

'How can we live without Heinz and Pappy?' I cried. 'Nothing matters now that they are gone.'

I had many similar outbursts. Sometimes Mutti didn't say anything, but could only give me a hug. Other times she offered comforting words and assured me that we would never stop loving Pappy and Heinz. She told me stories about my childhood, recollecting countless wonderful times. She reminded me of the courage and fortitude that Pappy had always fostered in us, and the smiles that Heinz had generated with his stories and music.

'They would want you to be happy, Evi,' Mutti said.

She was right. Although Pappy and Heinz were gone, all that they shared with me still remained, and through the following years I felt a powerful connection to them that I could never fully explain.

Mutti surprised me with a visitor from London: a ray of hope during those dark days. I had not seen my cousin Gaby for almost eight years. At first we didn't know what to say, so much had happened since we were last together. Then all the words and tears came flooding out at once.

It was the first time I could talk and cry freely about Heinz. Gaby missed and loved him too.

She stayed for a couple of weeks. She helped me feel like myself again. We shopped for wooden shoes, dressed up as Dutch girls and took long walks at the seaside. Mutti took photos of us, elated to see me smiling again.

My life felt like a see-saw, up and down, up and down. Sometimes I laughed, sometimes I cried. My feelings were mixed up. At times I felt very old, and other times I was like a little girl, not a sixteen-year-old. I would wake up from nightmares, screaming until Mutti came to my side. She always stayed with me as long as I needed her.

For many months the things I had once enjoyed had very little meaning. I didn't notice the flowers in bloom or the boats on the canal. I had no desire to do anything – not even ride my bike. I heard music I had once enjoyed, but it was nothing more than sounds and I simply didn't care about it.

Then one afternoon I was walking past the square where my friends and I used to run and play. Out of an apartment window floated the melodies of George Gershwin, Heinz's favourite composer. When I closed my eyes it could have been him at our piano bringing the music to life. There he was before me, his fingers dancing across the keys, his eyes darting from the score to me flitting about the room. I felt his energy and joy reach out to me. But when I opened my eyes, the street was empty.

'Heinz, where have you gone?' I cried. 'You were always with me. You always helped me: when I was in trouble, when I was sad, when I was confused. What can possibly help me now?'

I held on to the railing beside me and sobbed until I had no more tears. I couldn't move from that spot for quite some time. At long last, when I was able to continue walking home, I felt somehow that Heinz's music was still with me.

Some days, when the sky was blue and the sun bright, I noticed small rays of hope; the kind Pappy drew our attention to when all the trouble began. He would look for the best in every situation. He explained that in life you must always hope for a better future, or you won't be able to carry on. Like a mountain-climber who does not surrender to the treacherous cliffs on his right and left, he encouraged me to move forward, to keep climbing.

Mutti and I visited the Reitsmas, remembering how amazing it was that they had been spared in exchange for Mutti's box of jewellery. Before our capture, Mutti had given them the key to the warehouse where we had stored our packages of food. They told us that these generous provisions had kept them alive during the terrible 'Hunger Winter' in Holland when others were left with nothing to eat except for the tulip bulbs.

'Nearly everything tasted like mothballs,' their son Floris explained, 'especially the chocolate. But we really didn't mind.'

Mutti shared her concerns about my moods with Mrs Reitsma. I had refused to join in any parties or go out with friends. I was constantly studying to the point of exhaustion, so I didn't have extra time to think. Mrs

Reitsma was an artist and she suggested that perhaps it would help me to do some painting. So we made up a schedule and I began to take lessons from her. While I worked on my compositions, she worked on a new project. Mrs Reitsma, who was renowned for her etchings, had been commissioned to design a stamp commemorating the liberation of Holland.

Notices had been posted all over the city about the few people who had returned to Amsterdam. Otto Frank had seen our names and came to our apartment to visit. I had thought about him a couple of times since finding him in Auschwitz after the Nazis left. He and Mutti talked for a long time. He seemed to be in a desperate state. Sadly, he told us that his wife had been killed in Auschwitz, and his daughters, Margot and Anne, had died from typhus in Bergen-Belsen concentration camp. Margot had been Heinz's age; Anne, my age. Mutti told him about Heinz and Pappy, and somehow it helped them both to share their grief.

One day Mr Frank arrived with a little parcel under his arm. He opened it very carefully, yet eagerly. It was a diary that he had given Anne for her thirteenth birthday. She had written in it faithfully throughout the two years his family had been in hiding. He read a few passages to us, but was too emotionally caught up in his daughter's words to read more. He had a look of peace on his face, and it was the first time I saw the familiar charm I remembered from the days before the war. Through Anne's diary, he felt that she was still really with him. This treasure of her thoughts, ideas and dreams was like a lifeline for him.

Mr Frank became Mutti's friend and confidant. He helped her with my problems, as I had become a difficult teenager. Since his own daughters were gone, he became like a father to me. I didn't believe I could live an ordinary life and I had trouble making friends. I couldn't block the horrific memories out of my mind, and I had to deal with seeing images of what had happened all the time.

Mutti reminded me that we had to make a choice. We could choose to despair, or we could find a reason to go on. She and Mr Frank became active in the repatriation programme, helping many individuals and families resettle and begin their lives again. They were a great comfort to others, despite their own losses. Their generosity and kindness reminded me of Pappy's big-heartedness.

Then, one day, I suddenly remembered the whispered conversation I'd had with Heinz on the train journey to Auschwitz about the paintings he'd done, and how he'd hidden them. After hearing about Anne's diary and the way it had made Mr Frank feel closer to Anne, I thought perhaps Heinz's paintings would help Mutti and I feel closer to him.

'Heinz told me that he and Pappy hid their paintings under the floorboards when they were with Mrs DeBruin,' I told Mutti anxiously. 'He said that he left a note saying he would retrieve them after the war. Can we go, Mutti? Heinz would have wanted us to have them.'

Mutti listened intently. She was encouraged by my excitement, and finally agreed.

The DeBruins' house was outside Amsterdam. It felt strange to board the train and walk through the streets without a worry, with no soldiers, no reason to be afraid. When we arrived at the house, we were surprised to find a young couple living in the house. We explained the situation and told them about the paintings, but they became suspicious of our motives and stated that they didn't want to get involved.

Mutti and I stood on the doorstep, stunned. I was heartbroken.

'Oh, please, you must believe us. It is all we have left –'

'Maybe we should come back another time,' Mutti interrupted, 'and give these people a chance to think about our request,' she added hopefully.

She took my arm and turned as if to walk away, then stopped and looked back. 'The paintings were very special to my son, and now he is gone,' she said simply. 'Please, can't you understand how much this means to me and my daughter?'

The young man's hand was on the doorknob. He turned to his wife, whose face had taken on a gentler, softer look.

'I suppose I don't know how anyone could come up with such a peculiar story,' he said. 'You'd better come in.'

We sat on the floor underneath the attic window, as Heinz had described to me. My heart began to race as I touched the wood that Pappy had nailed down. It had been only a year and a few months since Heinz knelt on that very spot.

What was Heinz thinking when he and Pappy decided to hide the paintings? I wondered. *Did they imagine what it*

would be like for Mutti and me to come back without them?
What if the paintings were damaged during this time, or even
destroyed? What if someone took them? Oh, please let them be
there.

Mutti carefully lifted the floorboards, and the daylight revealed a priceless treasure. One by one, she slowly took them out. I wanted to wrap my arms around them.

'Oh, look, Evi. Heinz's sailing boat,' Mutti said in a shaky voice. She held up the painting for everyone to see.

'They're lovely,' the couple said together.

We found thirty in all. Some of Heinz's paintings reminded me of happy times and places: our family supper table; a couple playing a game of tennis; Heinz hoisting his sail. Some were very sad: a deserted attic; a lonely, dark corridor.

Pappy had completed two portraits: Mutti with her head bowed low and sad; Mutti, loving and kind, with the weight of the world in her eyes.

I was overcome with a longing for the past, for Heinz's stories, dreams and laughter. I missed Pappy's reassuring voice, his strong hands, his clever ideas, his gentle teasing. I vowed never to forget his loving promise: *Everything you do leaves something behind; nothing gets lost. All the good you have accomplished will continue in the lives of the people you have touched. It will make a difference to someone, somewhere, sometime, and your achievements will be carried on. Everything is connected, like a chain that cannot be broken.*

Then my eyes rested on the last picture Mutti uncovered. Heinz had painted himself, studying at his desk by an oil lamp, as he so loved to do. A calendar hung on the wall beside him. It was marked 11 May – my birthday! I cried with the realization that in that moment his thoughts were of me. He had brought us together once more. When my tears were finally spent, I felt exhausted but light. My heart filled with an immense thankfulness for all that Heinz and Pappy had given me that could never be taken away.

12.

Called to a New Horizon

Mutti and Mr Frank felt that I needed a fresh start, a new horizon that would help me leave the past behind. I was extremely restless in Holland. I felt very bitter and found it difficult to trust others. Fortunately, I encountered people like Dr Gunning, the headmaster at the *Lyceum* where Heinz had attended. I had missed three whole years of school, yet Dr Gunning helped me greatly with encouragement and generosity. He gave me and the few other Jewish students who returned extra lessons so that we could catch up with the other children our age. He even brought us extra food, which was still being rationed.

Mr Frank was also very helpful and loving towards me. I began to feel like he was a member of our family. He invited me to start calling him Otto. He was always willing to talk about things and inspired me to look optimistically towards the future. He didn't seem to harbour any feelings of bitterness or resentment.

'Look around,' he often said. 'You will see that there is a lot of good in people, and you can always find new things to learn and appreciate.'

It was a slow process, but I began to notice small acts

of kindness and thoughtfulness and grew more comfortable with other people.

Mutti and I visited England in the summer of 1946. We stayed with Mutti's sister, Aunt Sylvi, who still ran a snack bar and worked long hours, while Grandmother looked after Tommy, already ten years old! Uncle Otto, Aunt Sylvi's husband, was still overseas in the Czech army. Everyone was very anxious for him to come home. Grandfather still played piano in the pubs around Lancashire to the great enjoyment of all the patrons. Although I was no longer a little girl, he still invited me to walk with him like we had done on Sunday mornings in Vienna.

I liked England. Many refugees had been welcomed there, and I could imagine adapting to the British culture. Otto contacted a friend in London who gave me a job at her large photo studio. I moved there for a year in the summer of 1950, shortly after turning twenty-one.

Contrary to my nature, I felt somewhat reserved and shy in such a big city. I had never seen an underground train, and was not very comfortable with the English language. I had to travel forty-five minutes on the Underground to my place of work. I loved being part of thousands of people rushing around going to different places. My colleagues were all young and very poor, like me. We took turns buying a daily newspaper costing one penny, and read it in turn.

I enjoyed my job. As I became more familiar with the

play of light and colour in the images I captured, I felt a special closeness to Heinz. It made me happy to think how he would have commented on my work, encouraging and praising my efforts.

I boarded in a small lodging house run by a Czech refugee named Mrs Hirsch. She became very protective towards me, because all of the other lodgers were young men. One quickly became a good friend. His name was Zvi Schloss, a handsome, clever and very intelligent economics student from Israel. His family had fled Germany after his father was released from a concentration camp at Dachau.

Zvi liked to read and enjoyed talking about serious topics; unlike me, he was not a bit sporty. He often reminded me of Heinz, with a book in his hands. His appearance somewhat resembled Pappy, but not his character. Zvi was quiet and reserved. He seemed lonely, having been in England only a short time. I started going for long walks with him, and we got on very well. In time our relationship grew.

Zvi's experiences had been quite different from mine and he couldn't really understand all that I had been through, but his presence was a great comfort to me. I admired his views and appreciated his wisdom about life. He enjoyed my athletic ability and laughed when I walked on my hands or tried the fancy dives that Pappy had taught me. I began to realize that we belonged together, that we had a future to look forward to.

Zvi and I became engaged during a holiday at the seaside in northern England. We married in Amsterdam in 1952, with Grandmother Helen, Mutti, Otto and Zvi's mother in attendance. It was a simple wedding, and Grandmother, Mutti and I all wore light spring-coloured suits. Zvi and I moved to northwest London, where I had great fun turning a drab little apartment into a friendly place with flowers and inexpensive prints on the wall. Zvi was very impressed with all my efforts.

In later years I opened an antique shop, searching for treasures like I had done before with Pappy in Vienna. I collected paintings of beautiful children, hoping to have a big family of my own. One day Grandmother surprised me with the little Buddhist temple Pappy had bought at an auction in Vienna. She had included it in the few possessions transported to England in 1939. It brought back very special memories.

Life was good again, and Zvi and I dreamed of having children of our own who could share in our happiness. In 1956 our first daughter, Caroline Anne, was born. The whole family celebrated with great rejoicing the beginning of a new generation, a sign that our family did, in fact, continue. Caroline, with her big beautiful eyes, charmed everyone. Otto often called her Anne, as she brought back fond memories of his own daughter.

Two years later Jacky was born, named after my only real friend in Brussels. She captured others with her sweet, engaging smile. She looked at me with trusting eyes that healed my wounds of mistrust. In 1962 we welcomed our third daughter, Sylvia, named after Aunt Sylvi. She longed to understand her roots, inspiring me to return to Austria, to walk again in the places where I'd spent my early childhood.

Mutti also looked towards a new horizon when she and Otto fell in love. They were married in 1953, and provided wonderful support and companionship for each other through the years. They devoted their lives to promoting Anne's diary, and spread a message of peace and hope to others. They visited people of all ages at schools and in cities everywhere that grew to love Anne through her writing. They received thousands of letters from all over the world and answered every single one. Even during visits to my family in England, they spent hours tucked away in a spare room working on their correspondence. This really became their life.

I have never seen a happier marriage, and I was extremely happy for Mutti, although deep down, I always felt a stab of pain that someone had taken the place of my father. Nonetheless, Otto was a very good stepfather to me and a loving grandfather to my three daughters. He took them on his lap when they were little and often told them stories, the same as he'd told Margot and Anne.

At the end of every year we met Mutti and Otto in Switzerland for a skiing holiday. Otto organized an early evening New Year's party for all the children in the hotel. Those who didn't have any brothers or sisters were particularly thrilled to be included. He and Mutti purchased all kinds of prizes for the games they planned: chocolates, packs of cards and little trinkets. After hours of fun, when it was time for the adults' New Year's dance to begin, the children went to bed, happy and tired.

Otto died in 1980 at ninety-one years of age. Mutti lived to enjoy all five of her great-grandchildren. Jacky's daughter, Lisa, is the first: strong-willed, determined and motherly like Grandmother Helen. The second is her brother, Eric, a sports fanatic like Pappy, but with the gentleness of Heinz. I often feel close to Heinz in their midst. Caroline's only son, Alex, is third, always one to stick up for the underdog. He has loved Judaism from a very young age, and joyfully celebrated his bar mitzvah at thirteen like many Jewish boys. His father described this special event as 'a celebration of the continuation of the chain of Jewish life'. Sylvia's daughters are the fourth and fifth great-grandchildren. Sophie, the elder, draws constantly, writing and illustrating her own stories. Ella, the youngest, often has a book in her hands; yet she also likes to learn how to fix things, just like me.

I have had many joys throughout my life, more than I could ever have imagined, and yet there have been periods of great sadness as well. I have continued to miss Pappy and Heinz. I wanted my children to know their Grandfather Erich and their Uncle Heinz. Pappy died when he was only forty-four and Heinz before he would have turned eighteen. It took years and years for me to weave their absence into my life. Maybe things would have been different if I had witnessed their deaths. But they just disappeared, so it was much harder to accept.

Like many Jews, I lost my faith during the war. Yet when I started to begin a normal life again I had many questions and a growing appreciation for Judaism. I thought life would be really meaningless if you just lived and died, and that was the end of it all.

I looked at nature, I looked at my children and grandchildren and I thought, *It's really all so wonderful, so marvellous, there must be something higher. God must exist.*

I realized that my Jewish faith is a gift, and I would never change it. I believe that God was not responsible for the terrible tragedy of the Holocaust; that God gives us a free will and it is up to us to choose between good and evil. The Nazis chose evil and the whole world has suffered as a result.

My life turned towards a new horizon in 1986, forty-one years after the Second World War ended, when I finally shared my story. Initially, no one wanted to hear about the experiences of those who had survived the Holocaust. After all, everyone had suffered a great deal during the war. Some felt guilty that they had not done more to prevent the terrible atrocities. It was extremely painful to consider the extent of what had happened. From our homeland of Austria, hundreds of thousands of people perished, including my friend Kitty and her whole family. One and a half million people died at Auschwitz-Birkenau, and six millions Jews across Europe. But silencing the truth only caused everyone to suppress their emotions, which was particularly difficult for me. By the 1980s I felt the time was right to speak out and tell people about what had really happened.

My husband and friends were spellbound as I revealed the events of my childhood. By then, I was nearly sixty years old. While they were greatly shaken, they were also moved. This inspired me to write my book, *Eva's Story*. I wanted people to know the truth, so they could hopefully learn from it.

In 1995 James Still, an American playwright, interviewed me. He had conducted extensive research about the Holocaust and had been commissioned to write a play about the experiences of children whose lives touched Anne Frank. His play, entitled, *And Then They Came for Me: Remembering the World of Anne Frank*, encompasses much of my family's story. I attended the opening performance in New Brunswick, New Jersey, and was invited to come on stage afterwards to respond to questions from the audience. It was a powerful and unforgettable experience. This was the first time I met my penfriend from Michigan, Barbara Powers. We felt as if we had known each other all our lives.

At present I have attended more than nine hundred performances with many different production companies across America, in England, Australia, Latvia and Germany. To my great delight my childhood friend, Martin, who played with Heinz and me at our home in Vienna, arranged the performance in Australia. His family had escaped to Shanghai when Austria was invaded and eventually settled in Australia. During the very first performances I was in tears from start to finish.

I am always saddened by the magnitude of all that was lost during this period of my life. I am always struck by the message of the play, which underlines the dangers of prejudice and the need for tolerance. I am always moved by the warm welcome and genuine caring of both actors and audience in every theatre.

In sharing my story, I am able to celebrate Heinz and Pappy's life and the love of my family with people all over the world. Many of Heinz's paintings have been exhibited in cities around the USA. A permanent exhibition can be found in the Museum for the Resistance in Amsterdam. Two paintings hang in my home. They remind me that our moments together were precious. They inspire me to make the most of every gift I have been granted.

A Note from Barbara Powers

Imagine writing a book with one of your best friends, spending hours talking about all that has happened in your life, the good times and bad, cherished memories and memories you wish you could forget, your dreams and stories. This is how *The Promise* came about. It started with a friendship.

I first met Eva after suffering a personal tragedy. I listened in awe as she told about her experiences during the Holocaust, the horrendous events that erased whole families from the face of the earth, devastated a continent and overturned the world. I was amazed at how Eva's family endured and how she and her mother survived. I was deeply inspired by how they lived: how Pappy found reasons to be happy in the midst of fear and uncertainty; how Mutti focused on hope when surrounded by despair; and how Heinz brought beauty into sadness with his poetry, music, storytelling and painting.

Eva appreciates life to the full. Her energy for meeting new people, exploring new places and facing new challenges seems limitless. She even went parasailing at the age of seventy!

Eva has chosen not to harbour anger or bitterness. She shares her family's story in order to help others understand the results of intolerance, hatred and injustice, as well as the fruits of love and acceptance. She joins a multitude of men, women and children of all ages and backgrounds who long for a better world. May *The Promise* serve as a stepping stone in this direction.

Barbara Powers is a mother of five, living in mid-Michigan, with her children and husband, John. She is a graduate from Rutgers University, where she majored in Visual Art. Barbara works as a school curriculum coordinator, plays viola in a string quartet and frequently travels to visit her large extended family across the USA.

'Sad, matter of fact, harrowing and hopeful . . . a testament to the power of stories' – *Publishing News*

MORRIS GLEITZMAN

Everybody deserves to have something good in their life.

At least **Once.**

Once I escaped from an orphanage to find Mum and Dad.
Once I saved a girl called Zelda from a burning house.
Once I made a Nazi with toothache laugh.

My name is Felix. This is my story.

Discover the unforgettable new novel from bestselling and award-winning Morris Gleitzman.

Want to stay ahead of the game?

Then go online @ puffin.co.uk

- Extracts and info on all the latest books
- Exclusive author interviews
- Quizzes and competitions
- Screensavers and wallpapers
- Have your say and write reviews

You're only a mouse click away!

puffin.co.uk

Puffin by Post

he Promise – Eva Schloss and Barbara Powers

If you have enjoyed this book and want to read more,
then check out these other great Puffin titles.
You can order any of the following books direct with Puffin by Post:

Anne Frank's Story • Carol Ann Lee • 0141309261 Her life retold for children	£4.99
One Small Suitcase • Barry Turner • 0141314699 'A gem amongst non-fiction war books' – *The Times*	£5.99
Anne Frank and the Children of the Holocaust • Carol Ann Lee • 0141319631 The story of Anne Frank and the world in which she grew up	£5.99
Thura's Diary • Thura Al-Windawi • 0141317698 A young girl's life in war-torn Baghdad	£5.99
Chew On This • Eric Schlosser • 0141318449 Everything you don't want to know about fast food	£5.99

Just contact:

Puffin Books, C/o Bookpost, PO Box 29,
Douglas, Isle of Man, IM99 1BQ
Credit cards accepted. For further details:
Telephone: 01624 677237
Fax: 01624 670923

You can email your orders to: bookshop@enterprise.net
Or order online at: www.bookpost.co.uk

Free delivery in the UK.
Overseas customers must add £2 per book.

Prices and availability are subject to change.

Visit puffin.co.uk to find out about the latest titles, read extracts and
exclusive author interviews, and enter exciting competitions.
You can also browse thousands of Puffin books online.